Finding Financial Fulfillment

For a Life Filled with Money and Meaning

Janet Tyler Johnson

Goblin Fern Press
Madison, Wisconsin

Copyright © 2006 by Janet Tyler Johnson.

All rights reserved. No part of this book may be used or reproduced in any manner whatsoever without written permission, except in the case of brief quotations embodied in critical articles or reviews. For information, please contact the publisher.

Goblin Fern Press
6401 Odana Road, Suite B
Madison, WI 53719
Toll-free: 888-670-BOOK (2665)
www.goblinfernpress.com

Library of Congress Cataloging-In-Publication Data

Johnson, Janet Tyler.
Finding financial fulfillment :
for a life filled with money and meaning /
Janet Tyler Johnson.
p. : ill., charts ; cm.

Includes bibliographical references.
ISBN-13: 978-1-59598-040-3
ISBN-10: 1-59598-040-7

1. Finance, Personal. 2. Self-realization. I. Title.

HG179 .J64 2006
332.024/01

Printed in the United States.

*To my husband Randy,
who every day, in every way,
encourages me to live the life
of my dreams.*

Table of Contents

Acknowledgements vii
Introduction xiii

1. What is Financial Fulfillment? 17
2. What do You Value? 25
3. Creating Your Ideal Life 39
4. What Gets in Our Way? 55
5. Does Your Spending Support Your Ideal Life? 75
6. Creating More Abundance in Our Lives 89
7. Finding More Time to Do the Things
   that Fulfill Us 109
8. Building a Solid Financial Foundation 129
9. Understanding Investing Fundamentals 153
10. Teaching Our Children about Financial
    Fulfillment 167
11. Summing It All Up! 179

Acknowledgements

This book would never have made its way from my heart to print without the love, encouragement, and undying support of my husband, Randy. I bestow upon him my eternal love and deepest gratitude.

My parents, Dave and Lois Tyler, gave me not only every opportunity to live the life of my dreams while I was growing up, but continue to be a source of great love and encouragement, no matter where life takes me. They also gave me the most wonderful example of living out their dreams. They have always been and continue to be great role models.

Both my business and this book were birthed with the help of two great women in my life, Kira Henschel, owner of Goblin Fern Press, my book coach, editor and publisher, and Janet Ady, owner of

Voltedge, Inc., my branding and marketing guru. In addition to being wonderful friends, they both saw my vision and helped me create it. To both of them and their fabulous employees, I express my deepest gratitude.

To Bob Veres, my heartfelt thanks in reading my manuscript. His expertise in the world of the written word as an author, an editor, and a journalist, and his knowledge of the financial services industry made him the perfect choice to be an early reader. I am proud to call this man a friend and so appreciate his kindness and assistance.

To Paul Ditscheit: energy healer, teacher, and friend. Words cannot express the gratitude I have for Paul! I wouldn't be where I am today without him.

To my clients, I express my ongoing gratitude for the faith and confidence they have shown me. Their appreciation for the part I play in their lives has inspired me to be the best that I can be. It doesn't get any better than that!

To Tracy Beckes, my coach, my friend, and my mentor I express my heartfelt thanks for her dedication to authenticity. She has taught me to dig deeper and deeper so I can reach the stars. She has helped me in ways that are too numerous to mention.

To all of the members of the New Glarus "Light the Night Leukemia Walk" committee, I thank them from the bottom of my heart for all they have done to take an idea and turn it into a miracle. I especially want to thank Roger and Karen Nodorft, Karla Heller, and Kellie Engelke for their willingness to lead the charge and their never-ending energy and enthusiasm for this great cause. They each have turned a tragedy in their own lives into hope for so many others. I am so honored to know each and every one of them.

To Laura Cardelli, my "other mom," who has been a blessing in my life, I thank her for her willingness to share her story and for all the encouragement she has given me over the years. She is the definition of "friend," and I will love her always.

To Carol Nowka, who truly is a role model as a Certified Financial Planner® professional and as a woman. I thank her for sharing her story and for coming into my life. She has a heart of gold and it is a privilege to know her. I only wish I'd met her sooner!

To my sister and brother, Dr. Kathryn Tyler and Bruce Tyler, I express my sincere gratitude for all the support they have given me over the years, for all the great memories, and all the laughter they bring to our family. They are both a blessing! And to my brother-in-law, Ken Pacholski, my thanks for showing all of us the humor in everything.

My stepchildren, Steve, Kristin, and Stacia Johnson, have been a continuous source of love and joy. They have given me the gift of finding out first-hand what parenting is all about and I thank them for making that such a positive experience. I am so proud of each of them and look forward to watching their fabulous lives unfold.

To my niece, Rachel Tyler, my eternal gratitude. The news that she would soon be born (10 years ago) became the first of several Universal nudges for me to move to Wisconsin. It was the first time I consciously followed my intuition and it proved to be one of the best things I have ever done in my life. I have so enjoyed watching Rachel grow into a beautiful, intelligent, talented girl. I feel blessed to be part of her life.

To the entire Johnson family, I thank each and every one of them for welcoming me and making me feel part of their family from our first meeting. It has been a joy to be part of such a loving, talented, and kind group of people.

To all my friends in the Nazrudin Project who cheered me on as I established my own business. It is an honor to be associated with some of the best minds in the financial planning industry. I am humbled in their presence and eternally grateful to be counted among them.

And last, but not least, to my colleagues/buddies, who have an endless supply of talent, integrity and enthusiasm in an industry that sometimes seems to need more of all three: John Braeseke, Steve Mathias, and Tim McCain. I appreciate so much your friendship and your continued support of my endeavors.

—*Janet Tyler Johnson*

*Dream lofty dreams,
and as you dream,
so shall you become.*

*Your vision is the
promise of what you
shall at last unveil.*

—John Ruskin

Introduction

*T*his book is about having it all. About having the life of your dreams, about having everything you truly desire. It's about living a life where you get to the end of it and have absolutely no regrets.

Financial fulfillment means more than just creating wealth. It means having money AND meaning in your life. Having money for money's sake does not give anyone a sense of fulfillment. It often leaves a person feeling like there's something missing. And there is. But creating a life that is filled with meaning allows you to use money to serve you; you don't serve it.

Financial fulfillment does not mean, necessarily, that you need great wealth, nor does it mean that you need to forego wealth to lead the "simple" life. There is nothing wrong with having money (and some of us desire a great deal of money, not just for ourselves, but so we can improve the lives of others). To have fulfillment in your life, you will need to decide specifically what you want your life to look like. You need to know what is important to you, what you value, and what true fulfillment means to you. We will work through some simple exercises together to help you do that.

Once you've defined what you want your Ideal Life to look like, then we will look at whether your money is supporting each area of your life that you specify is important to you. If there is a shortfall (not enough income or assets to achieve your Ideal Life), we will discuss some strategies to attract more abundance to you.

The key is figuring out what makes you feel fulfilled and defining what is important to you—your values. This is a fun process, not an arduous one. It is a freeing process, not a confining one. It allows you to dream again, to explore possibilities, to remember what you truly value, and begin to live your life with more meaning. You will find, as others have, that once you've designed your fulfilling life, more and more positive things will happen to support you in achieving that life.

Sound too good to be true? It's not. The Universe wants you to succeed. So let's begin our journey.

The only peace, the only security, is in fulfillment.

—Henry Miller

Chapter 1

What is Financial Fulfillment?

Let's start by answering the question "What is fulfillment?" The dictionary says it is feeling content, gratified, or satisfied. I know that fulfillment goes a lot deeper than that. It is the feeling you get when you are living totally in the present moment. You feel alive and energized, yet peaceful and relaxed. You lose all track of time. You are immersed in the NOW. There are no thoughts of the past or worries of the future. You are conscious of only the present moment. You feel an immense amount of gratitude for what you have. You know you are living "on purpose." You feel passionate about life. You savor each and every moment. You feel bliss.

Want to try something really fun that embodies fulfillment? Go to your favorite grocery store and buy one of the ripest peaches that you can find. (You can try this with any of your favorite foods, but there's just something special about a peach!) Next, find ten minutes when you will be completely alone. Grab a napkin. Sit down in a comfortable place and close your eyes. Then do absolutely nothing except eat and enjoy this peach. Smell the peach. Really inhale and smell its aroma. Take a bite, slowly, while thinking of nothing but how this peach tastes. Savor this bite while noticing how the peach feels in your mouth. Continue to eat the peach slowly, thinking only of what you are experiencing, feeling the juice run down your chin, your throat, over your fingers, until you have finished every last bite.

That, my friend, is a feeling of fulfillment.

Maybe a feeling of fulfillment for you happened when you first held your brand new baby, or watched a sunrise (or sunset), or were awed at the sight of the Grand Canyon, or played with a new puppy. The list could go on and on, but the common denominator in all of these examples is that you were living in the present moment, not in the past, nor worrying about the future. You felt whole. You felt joy! Deep, deep joy! Can you remember a time when you felt fulfilled?

A time in my own life when I truly felt a sense of fulfillment came about five years ago. I had been sponsoring a child in Brazil with a $25 per month charitable donation to him and his family. That particular year I sent him an extra $25 for Christmas. About two months later, I received a letter from him telling me all of the things his mother purchased with that $25. She bought, quoting from his letter, "two trunks, one blouse, two underclothes, and a toy for me. With the rest of the money my mother bought food supplies, such as flour, rice, sugar, coffee, cookies, macaroni, beans, greens, meat, and fruits. She also bought hygiene products, such as perfume, shampoo, toilet soap, and hair cream."

Never in my wildest imagination did I think my $25 check would go that far. I felt so wonderful knowing I could make such a huge difference in the life of another human being. For me, it became very evident that part of my Ideal Life had to contain an element of giving to others. And not just monetarily. My little Brazilian boy also expresses to me in every letter he writes how much he loves to hear from me. I send him pictures of our home surrounded by snow. He has never seen snow. And I send him pictures of my two dogs. He loves getting these. In return, he usually draws me a picture, which is proudly displayed on my refrigerator!

Because of this experience, I now have the intention to create more abundance in my life, so that I can continue to do things like that for others.

Financial fulfillment comes from having defined what fulfillment is for you, and then using your money to help you gain more of that fulfilling feeling. It's not about the money. *It's about the feeling.*

It's using your money to build a life filled with meaning and fulfillment. It's not about using money to alleviate boredom (overspending) or out of guilt (I don't have enough time with my kids, so I buy them things to make up for it). Nor is it spending money unconsciously. (Have you ever walked into a store, bought some things, and by the time you got to the car to go home, you forgot what was in the bag? That's spending money unconsciously!) In order to build a life that is oozing fulfillment, you have to know where your money is going and you have to feel that you have a firm financial foundation in place.

Janet Tyler Johnson

Worrying about your finances will never allow you to feel a sense of fulfillment. You have to put money in its rightful place; it needs to be supporting your vision for a life filled with fulfillment. You don't become a slave to money; you let money serve you. You decide what a really meaningful, fulfilling life would look like to you, and then you put your money to work to make that happen.

The clients I have worked with over the past 25 years who are the most fulfilled financially have all figured out for themselves what is most important to them, i.e., what they value, and then stopped spending money on the "stuff" that didn't matter. This allowed them to live the lives of their dreams that more quickly. They focused their time, energy, and resources solely on what was really important to them and no longer spent money for any other reason.

For most people, letting go of the "stuff" that doesn't matter is the easy part. It just happens as a by-product of gaining clarity about what our Ideal Life looks like. If you can get really clear on what you want, the rest just seems to happen.

The business owners I have worked with who have had long-term success and feel the most fulfillment in their lives placed "making money" somewhere in the middle or near the bottom of their list of goals. They were driven more by the desire to do work they love and provide a high-quality product or service to benefit others. Yes, they wanted to make money, but again, that wasn't the number one priority. It was the by-product or end result of putting their hearts and souls into a venture they felt passionate about.

When was the last time you felt passionate about your work—or your life for that matter? If your answer to that question is "I don't remember" or "I've never felt that way," then keep reading.

Most people don't feel fulfilled in their lives, and my passion lies in trying to change that. I don't want you to spend the rest of your life always feeling like you need more. Wanting more is OK, but feeling as if you were lacking something in some way isn't. I want to help you enjoy each and every day. I've seen too many people postpone their dreams "until the kids go back to school" or "until my luck changes" or "until I lose that 30 pounds" or until they reach "retirement" or some other specific time in their lives.

What if we don't live long enough to get there? What will we have missed out on in life? Why shouldn't we be able to treasure each and every day that we have on this Earth?

You deserve to have the best life possible. No matter where you are in life today, you have the power to change things for the better.

It's not as difficult as you think. There are some universal laws that are not only there to assist you, but the Universe itself is on your side and wants you to succeed. But it's up to you to begin.

The secret to living a more fulfilling life is to a) have a very clear picture of what you want your life to look like, and b) use your money to support that picture. Again, money should serve you; you shouldn't be serving it.

I speak from experience. For years I thought if I made enough money, I would feel fulfilled. I didn't. I re-evaluated and found that by spending my time living my Ideal Life, as I am today, not only am I feeling more fulfilled, I'm attracting even greater amounts of abundance into my life.

If you're willing to be honest with yourself and take the time needed to explore some things with me, we'll get to a place where not only your financial life improves, so does your entire life. And I promise you you'll be amazed at how wonderful your life can be.

If money is your is your motivation, forget it!

—Oprah Winfrey

Chapter 2

What Do You Value?

*F*inding financial fulfillment means aligning your money with your values. So how do you determine what your values are? What is important to you? What do you value in life? What things truly add to your life? Sometimes our biggest struggle is just figuring out what it is we really want; what REALLY matters to us. If we can identify those things and then put our money only toward what we value, we'll achieve our goals more quickly and gain far more satisfaction in life.

A few years ago I was introduced to one of the simplest methods I have ever seen to help you

Authentic values are those by which a life can be lived, which can form a people that produces great deeds and thoughts.

—Allan Bloom

Janet Tyler Johnson

"figure things out." It's called Mind Mapping and was developed by Tony Buzan, the originator of Mind Maps® and author of The Mind Map® Book. His book goes into great detail on the research behind this method, but I've found it very simple to do and a lot of fun. It can be applied to many, many things in your personal or business life.

Let me show you how it works.

First, you have a topic to brainstorm. As an example, let's say you want to buy a new home. Take "Home" and put it in a circle on a large piece of blank (not lined) paper. Copy paper or sketch paper works well for these exercises but feel free to get creative. Sometimes the larger the piece of paper, the better. Anything smaller than 8½ X 11 usually doesn't work as well, but once you get the hang of it, a match book cover will do the trick.

So, putting your topic in the circle in the middle of the paper would look like this:

Then, with lines coming off the circle, let's brainstorm the types of rooms you would like in this home:

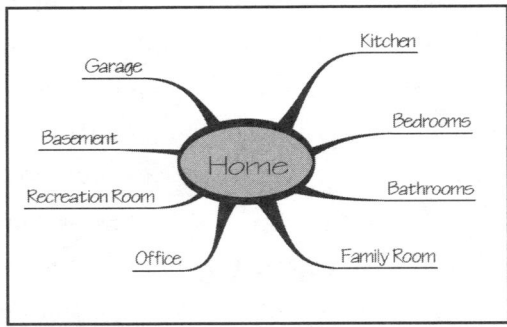

Let's get a little more detailed. By brainstorming what we'd want to do or have in our kitchen, the next part of our mind map could look like this:

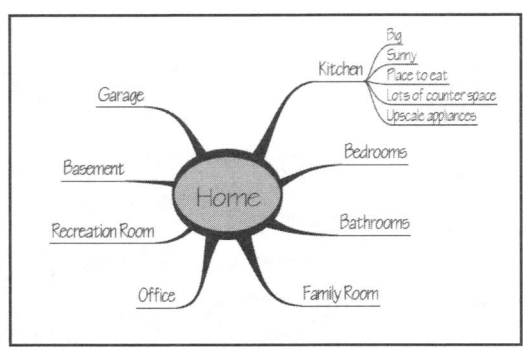

Janet Tyler Johnson

You get the idea; you can get this level of detail, and more, for each topic, subtopic, etc. If you spend some time on this, you will get a very clear picture of exactly what you want your home to look like.

Now let's apply this mind mapping technique to brainstorm your values. I'd like you to create separate mind maps for the following scenarios, in the order presented. (Trust me, there's a method to my madness here!) Again, these work best on plain paper with no lines. There are also some blank pages at the back of this book for you to use if you wish. Get a pencil, colored pencils, crayons, markers, whatever feels right to you. Have some fun with this. And don't worry about whether you're artistic or not. This is so easy you don't need any special talents—just have fun!

Here's Scenario #1:

> You have purchased a lottery ticket and just found out that you have won $100 million. What would you change about your life?"

Put "$100 million" in a circle in the middle of the page and then brainstorm all of the things that you would do with your life having just won this amount of money. Think about this for a while. You've got $100 million. What would you do? Here are some things to think about:

- Would you quit your job?
- Would you start a business?
- Would you pay for all or part of your children's or grandchildren's education?
- Would you travel the world?
- Would you create a foundation or give money to your favorite charity?
- Would you buy a different home? Or homes?
- Would you live in a different part of the country or world?
- Would you buy a Ferrari?
- Would you hire a maid?

I'd like you to spend at least ten minutes on this, longer if you can, and get as detailed as possible. Put on some relaxing music and pour yourself a nice, hot cup of tea. If it's a warm summer day, sit outside in the sun, or in the shade of a large tree. Make this a relaxing time, without interruptions, so you can really pour yourself into this.

After you complete this scenario, move on to Scenario #2:

> You go to your doctor and he says he has good news and bad news for you. The bad news is that you will be dead five years from today; the good news is that you will live symptom-free for the entire five years. Now, knowing that you have only five years left to live, what would you do differently with your life?

Put "5 years" in a circle in the middle of the page and then brainstorm what you would do, knowing you only have five years left to live. Again, spend *at least* ten minutes on this, and if you think you're done, spend a little more time and try to see if anything else comes to you.

Lastly, we have Scenario #3:

> The doctor was wrong. You don't have five years left to live, you only have 24 hours. If you were to die 24 hours from now, what would you ***regret not having done in your life***?

Finding Financial Fulfillment

This time put "24 hours" in the circle and brainstorm as many things as possible that you would regret not having done if you were to die 24 hours from now. What things have you always wanted to do that you've been putting off? What would you have done with your life if you *knew* you couldn't fail? You get the idea.

After completing all three scenarios, what do you notice? Make a note of any impressions you get. Did you gain any clarity into what you REALLY value in life?

If you spend enough time on mind mapping these scenarios, some really powerful things will happen. I worked with one client who first did these exercises in a workshop I held. Clara was 45 and single with no children. She had a niece who was ten years old at the time. During the first scenario with the $100 million, she had no problem listing all of the "stuff" she would buy: the new house, a second home, new cars, a boat, new furniture, new clothing, traveling to many exotic places. Can you relate to any of this?

During the second scenario she narrowed this list to a few places she really wanted to travel to and then focused more on her family—her sister and brother, her parents, and her niece. Knowing she had a definite timeframe caused her to look at things that she valued as more important in her life than a new house or car or clothes.

It was the third scenario, however, that really opened her eyes. Clara was an attorney who worked in a local law firm. She enjoyed her work yet when she thought about what she'd regret, she immediately realized that she had always wanted to start her own catering business. For a variety of reasons, she had just never done it.

We began talking at length about her desire to open a business and really explored whether it was something that would make her life more enjoyable. While she enjoyed her work as an attorney, it had never felt as fulfilling as planning a party and cooking for others did. She loved hosting big parties, whether they were formal affairs or casual backyard barbecues. Her guests always raved about her food and the way she presented it.

She had dreamed of catering weddings, graduation parties, anniversary parties, and corporate bashes. She had ideas for all types of events and some of her ideas were even written down. She could see herself handling all the details, from the planning stage, to the cooking, to hiring the right people to serve as wait

Finding Financial Fulfillment

staff. She dreamt of having her own place of business that would include beautiful office space to meet with clients and a large commercial kitchen to handle all the food prep needs.

Clara had even saved some money over the years that could be used to help start this venture. She realized through completing these mind maps that she would gain more fulfillment in her life by doing work that she really loved. Now it was time to start putting her money toward her vision.

What old dreams have you forgotten about? What did you love to do when you were a kid? What are things you do where you lose all track of time when you're doing them? What makes you feel alive, really alive? If you could go back and do it all over again, what would you do differently? What do you like to do in your free time? What's your favorite hobby? What are you talented at? What do other people think you're great at? (If you don't know, ask them.) If you were given the gift of a year off and money wasn't an issue, how would you spend your time?

Ponder these questions. There are clues here.

For some of us, the hardest part is trying to figure out what we really want our life to look like. We're too busy just trying to get through today. Despite all of today's technology and inventions that were intended to make our lives easier, life has gotten more complicated for most of us. How did we all get so busy?

I'd like to suggest that you take out a daily planner and write down what your typical day looks like. Be sure to include all your activities during the day, not just business appointments. If you really want to see something amazing, write out what an entire week looks like. Is this the way you want your life to look in the future?

We live in a reactive society. We're constantly reacting to things that need our attention. To get off this merry-go-round for good, we need to decide what is truly important to us and stop doing the stuff that isn't. But the first step is deciding what we want our life to look like. If you're not willing to take the time to do this and get a clear picture in your head (and drawn out and hung on your wall), don't expect your life to change. If you haven't done it already, make the time to go back through this chapter and do the exercises, ponder the questions, try to get clarity on what you want out of life.

Just reading about it won't get it done. I'd even like to suggest that you go so far as to turn your mind maps into large wall hangings. Feel free to add photos from magazines or drawings. Get creative. Keep your dreams in front of you. Don't take your eye off your desires. It will make things that much easier for your dreams to come true.

If I hadn't taken the time to create my own maps, this book would not have been written. I actually created a separate mind map just for this book. In about twenty minutes I had all the topics for the chapters laid out. I changed the title once, but that's OK. I just created a new map. I used the mind map as I wrote and added to it when I had new ideas. It became the road map for my journey.

Since preparing that map, I've created one map that is my "Ideal Life" map, another that is my business plan, and others on ideas that I want to implement in my business. It's amazing how I can now crank out a map in a matter of minutes. And that map is so much more powerful than just a list of ideas. It's a picture, and as you know, a picture is worth a thousand words. Personally, I think that's an understatement.

I know having a clear picture of what I want, that I am excited about, sets the wheels in motion for me to receive it. That, my friend, is priceless!

If you want your life to change for the better, spend some time thinking about the questions I've asked. Create mind maps to answer all of them. Use crayons or colored pencils, pictures and diagrams. Have fun with these exercises. I promise you, it will be worth every minute you put into this. I've seen some maps that others have done that are far more artistic than mine. If you love to draw, go all out. Create anything you want. Make them as elaborate or plain as you wish. It won't matter in the big scheme of things. My maps are very plain, drawn out with a pencil, but they are still powerful.

So whether you're artistic or not, just do it! Get that picture. Then we can go on to creating that life you've just put to paper.

The difference between great people and everyone else is that great people create their lives actively, while everyone else is created by their lives, passively waiting to see where life takes them next. The difference between the two is the difference between living fully and just existing.

—Michael E. Gerber

CHAPTER 3

Creating Your Ideal Life

Something magical happens for me whenever I get real clarity about something. It's like the light bulb going on. I get energized. It's an "aha" moment. If it's a project I'm working on, the minute I get clarity, I can't wait to get going on it and have a hard time putting it away. I'm in "the zone" and it feels great. When writing, for example, when I'm inspired, I can write for hours. I lose all track of time as my fingers just keep flying across the keyboard.

Many people I've talked to can't imagine writing a book because they think back to high school or college when they were forced to write papers on subjects they really didn't care very much about. However, when you're writing something you're passionate about, it's entirely different, at least for me. I feel very alive and in the present moment. No worries, no problems, just clear inspiration.

How do we get more clarity in our lives? I've found that I need to meditate for a few minutes, or just stop thinking and let things be, and suddenly an answer will appear. For the first forty years of my life, I had a really hard time shutting off my brain. I'd read a lot about meditating, but for me, it was difficult to not think. I'm a thinker, an analyzer, always trying hard to mentally figure something out, and usually, the harder I tried to think my way through things, the worse things got.

Then I met several teachers, some authors, and some healers who taught me to try "feeling" my way through something versus "thinking" my way through it. Sound like a foreign language? Well, it can be, but it's the most wonderful and most reliable foreign language I've ever learned.

Let me give you an example of this from my own life. My husband and I live in an area where each homeowner has a multi-acre lot. Most of these lots are heavily wooded. It's a very rural area out in the middle of nowhere, which made it very afford-

Janet Tyler Johnson

able for us. The entire surrounding area is beautiful rolling hills with small quaint towns and miles and miles of farmland. It's quiet and peaceful where the deer, raccoons, wild turkeys, and other wild birds abound. For us, it's like being "on retreat" every day and is the ideal place for us to live.

As we began building our dream home, it didn't take long to discover that, on our entire piece of property, we didn't have one flat area anywhere. It's beautiful to look at but a challenge at times when trying to decide things like "So where should the house go?" or "Where do we put the driveway or garage?"

We've lived here for over five years now and both my husband and I have experienced that the best answers to these questions have come through what we call "moments of divine inspiration." We've come to believe truly in the Universe for these answers, since experience has shown us that the best solutions have just "popped into our heads" one day.

We recently decided to put up a building near our house, part of which would be my office and the rest my husband's shop. Selecting the site was not a simple process. We couldn't come up with the right place for it to go. We even had a building contractor come out and he couldn't find an appropriate spot.

Finding Financial Fulfillment

Then one morning, upon waking, I looked out our bedroom window and BAM, it hit me. There was the perfect spot. I could see it. I told my husband and saw the immediate agreement on his face, like the light bulb went on. On the surface it may sound like this was a pretty insignificant event but our environment is very important to us. We knew we'd be living with where the building was located for the rest of our lives.

So how does this relate to creating the Ideal Life? Well, I know I'm on track when things FEEL right. I've learned to ignore my mind a great deal of the time because it is a master of rationalization, justification, and deception. I'd like you to keep this in mind as we go through some more creative exploration.

I call this the "Ideal Life Wheel™," as it contains areas you may want to look at when creating your Ideal Life. Let's spend a few minutes discussing each of the components. I would suggest doing a mind map for each of these topics. Then we'll do a final mind map called "My Ideal Life" that will incorporate all these maps into one.

Here are some ideas for each category.

Relationships:
This area encompasses your spouse, children, parents, siblings, other relatives, friends, co-workers, employees, employer, etc. A mind map might include the following topics:

Finding Financial Fulfillment

I want...
- A great relationship with my spouse/partner
- A great relationship with my children
- A great relationship with my parents
- Siblings who are also my best friends
- Joy-filled family gatherings
- A house filled with pets
- Friends I can trust and rely on
- People who help me grow as a person
- People who take joy in my success
- People I can give back to
- People who share my values
- People of other cultures

These are just some ideas. You need to determine what your Ideal Relationships might look like.

Work:
Let's forget about work in the traditional sense for a minute. Instead of thinking of what your ideal "job" would be, let's think of things like the following: What thing or things do you do where you absolutely lose all track of time when you are doing them? For example:
- Playing tennis or another sport
- Gardening
- Playing with your kids or grandkids
- Driving

Janet Tyler Johnson

- Dancing
- Playing a musical instrument
- Knitting
- Talking with people
- Reading
- Shopping (clothes, jewelry, cars, food)
- Cooking
- Working on a project
- Writing
- Drawing
- Hiking
- Bicycle riding
- Having meaningful conversations
- Helping others

When you find some things you are passionate about (losing track of time while doing them is usually a sign) then you can create an ideal work life where you get paid to do some of these things. For example, if hiking is something you are passionate about, have you ever thought about being a guide into the Grand Canyon, or into the mountains? If playing a musical instrument is a passion, have you thought about joining a band, or playing professionally, or teaching, or writing your own music and putting together a CD?

If working on the computer is a passion, what type of business can you run or work in that uses computers? Maybe it's being a computer technician, or

Finding Financial Fulfillment

maybe it's being a graphic artist. If sports are your passion, can you make money as a professional, or coaching, become a sports writer or a sports commentator? There are so many possibilities today. Let your creative mind flow and see what you can come up with.

A woman I know loves to shop. She thoroughly enjoys looking at beautiful clothes, jewelry, shoes, etc. She took that passion for shopping and became a buyer for a major national department store. Now she gets paid to shop spending the company's money. How fun is that???

Play:
These are things you do simply for pleasure, such as attending a baseball game, or going on a cruise. Maybe it's dinner out with friends or working a crossword puzzle. These things relax you. They are fun. Mind map as many things as you can think of. Here are some more ideas:

※ Visiting a museum
※ Going to a movie
※ Ice skating
※ Swimming
※ Skiing

Janet Tyler Johnson

- Going on a picnic
- Taking the dog for a walk
- Playing cards
- Putting together a jigsaw puzzle
- Woodworking
- Surfing the net
- Watching TV
- Reading
- Playing a musical instrument
- Drawing
- Writing poetry
- Cooking
- Going to the farmer's market
- Traveling

These are things that you don't necessarily want to make a living at but they add joy and fulfillment to your life.

Spirituality:
Again, let's create a mind map of things you do to practice your religion or spirituality. Here are some examples to get you thinking:

- Attending a house of worship
- Reading scripture or holy books
- Reading spiritual books
- Practicing meditation
- Doing yoga

Finding Financial Fulfillment

- Praying
- Walking in nature
- Chanting
- Dancing
- Playing music
- Listening to music
- Spending time with your pets

Keep in mind that we are thinking about our Ideal Life. What things do you want to incorporate into your life to bring out your spiritual nature?

Health:

This category includes both your physical and emotional health. Here are some ideas:

- Walking daily for 30 minutes
- Jogging 2 to 3 miles per day
- Bike riding
- Eating only whole foods
- Taking supplements
- Annual physicals
- Prostate exams
- Breast exams
- Dental checkups
- Having a positive attitude
- Taking responsibility
- Deciding to be happy
- Feeling loved

Janet Tyler Johnson

- Loving others
- Having a support system
- Reading positive, uplifting books
- Feeling lighthearted
- Staying away from violent TV and movies
- No longer watching the news
- Laughing more often

Giving back:

Giving back involves donating your time, talents, and money to causes you feel need your assistance. This can entail everything from donating to your local church or house of worship, being involved in the community, raising money for research for diseases, setting up a foundation to donate money to various worthy causes, volunteering at the local hospital or homeless shelter, or singing Christmas carols at the local nursing home at the holidays. Even if you don't have money to give, you do have time and some type of talent that others can benefit from. Search your heart on this one and decide what you can do to round out your Ideal Life.

Finding Financial Fulfillment

Take some time and really play with these components, as you'll want to get as detailed as you can when creating your Ideal Life mind map. Keep in mind, you should be careful what you wish for; you just might get it!!!

When you gain real clarity on your Ideal Life and create a picture of what that will look like, you set in motion an intention to the Universe. This intention is something that you want and the Universe wants you to have it. There is a law of attraction at work here. You will attract into your life what you think about. Again. *You will attract into your life what you think about.* So let's create your picture, your Ideal Life, so you have a picture in front of you that you can think about as often as possible.

Take a new blank sheet of paper and mind map your "Ideal Life," putting that as the title of your map (in the middle) and then taking all of the components of your Ideal Life Wheel™, your relationships, work, play, etc., and create your map. If you're so inclined, use colored pencils or markers. Cut out pictures and paste them on your map.

If one of your dreams is to have a hot red sports car, draw it or get a picture of one and paste it on your map. If you'd like to ultimately make so much money

Janet Tyler Johnson

My Own Story of Creating My Ideal Life

Here's a story of something that happened to me not long ago that illustrates how the Universe supports you when you're on the right path. In 2004, I was finishing my fourth year of being in charge of the financial planning and investment management division of a large accounting firm. I had been recruited to this position to build the infrastructure needed to provide financial planning and investment management services to the firm's clients. We were highly successful in the years I was there, including in our second year being named one of the fastest growing registered investment advisory firms in the country.

In the fourth year of building this company within a company, I was beginning to feel depleted. A voice inside me kept encouraging me to go into business for myself. I wanted to spend my time doing things I felt passion for, like writing and speaking and working directly with clients, not attending meeting after meeting.

I knew I would need to save a substantial amount of money if I was going to go into business for myself, so I started saving everything I could. I also asked the Universe to help me find the money I would need if this indeed was the path I was supposed to follow. Within two days of asking the Universe for help, I received an offer in the mail to buy back some stock in an insurance company that I owned. About 15 years ago, when licensed as an insurance representative, I had received a few

Finding Financial Fulfillment

> shares of stock from a reorganization of a company that I had done some business with. I had put the stock certificate for these shares in a safe place and had not even thought about them for a while. The shares, according to the letter I received in the mail, were now worth about $1,500 and here I was getting an offer to buy them back for cash.
>
> Needless to say, I took them up on their offer and in a few weeks had a check in my hands for the money. This is a very common occurrence to anyone living their dreams who has asked for assistance from God, the Universe, their spiritual guides, or whomever they believe in. Magic happens, and usually so often it starts to become the norm.

that you can donate money for a new shelter for domestic abuse survivors, draw or get a picture of what you think that shelter could look like.

Remember, the clearer you get, the easier it is for the Universe to support you. The Universe has a hard time giving you something when you're vague about it, when it doesn't know what you really want! The Universe has everything you need. It is just waiting for a clear message from you of specifically what you want. So the secret here is to tell it. Put your intention out to the Universe and then let go and wait. You'll be amazed how the right people and circumstances appear to help you on your journey.

Let some magic into your life! Be clear about what you want your life to look like, decide to move in that direction, and just watch what happens. Dare to be amazed!

A man is literally what he thinks.

—James Allen,
author of *As a Man Thinketh*

CHAPTER 4

What Gets in our Way?

I heard a story a long, long time ago about twin brothers who grew up with an alcoholic father. The father was very verbally abusive when he was drunk. He constantly demeaned his children, telling them they were worthless, no-good kids who wouldn't amount to anything.

When the two boys were in their forties, they were interviewed. One brother had become a very successful business owner, had a loving relationship with his wife and children, and lived a life that was very fulfilling. The other brother was an alcoholic, could never keep a job, had no family life, and was generally very miserable.

*It isn't what you have,
or who you are,
or where you are,
or what you are doing
that makes you
happy or unhappy.
It is what you
think about.*

—Dale Carnegie

Janet Tyler Johnson

Someone asked both brothers why they thought they turned out the way they did. Both brothers answered, "Because of my father."

This story has stayed with me for decades because it told me that there was something different between these two brothers. What was it? They were twins, they grew up in the same environment, they were treated the same, they had the same opportunities and challenges. So how did their lives turn out so differently?

I believe they thought different thoughts. They had different beliefs. One brother believed he would succeed because there was no way he wanted to be like his dad, and every thought he had was about how he would overcome his circumstances and succeed. He believed he could do it and he did. The other brother had thoughts of hopelessness. He didn't think there was any way he could amount to anything. At some level, he believed all the garbage his dad told him.

I don't know for a fact that this story is true, although I've seen such family dynamics in children of alcoholics, but there is truth in the way the story played out. The outcome of the two brothers' lives had everything to do with the thoughts that played through their heads.

Finding Financial Fulfillment

Maharishi Mahesh Yogi, founder of the Transcendental Meditation Program, stated, "All that we are is the result of what we have thought. The mind is everything. What we think, we become." This is very important: *what we think, we become*. Our thoughts, therefore, affect our outcomes.

For example, let's say you're up for a promotion at work. You find out that the promotion is between you and two other people. All day long you think to yourself, "God, I'll never get this promotion. Fred has more experience than I do, and Jenny is so smart."

What are you doing to yourself here? You're actually creating the outcome that you're not going to get this promotion.

Now, some of us think this way for self-preservation. We think if we prepare ourselves for the worst, it will be that much easier to take if we don't get what we want. But do you see what kind of message you are putting out there? Whether you think it or say it aloud, you're putting out the message that you are never going to get the promotion. What do you think will happen?

Such negative thinking actually physically weakens you. Try this experiment: Ask a trusted friend to help you with this. Extend your left arm straight out

Janet Tyler Johnson

from your body so it is parallel to the floor, palm down. Now ask your friend to place his first two fingers on top of your wrist. Both of you close your eyes. Have your friend ask you your name. Lie and state a name that isn't yours. At the same time, have your friend push down on your arm.

No matter how hard you push up, he will easily be able to move your arm down with just two fingers. Now, try it again, but this time state the truth and your correct name. Have him push down on your wrist again. He will not be able to move your arm. Both of you will see the difference in the strength of your arm.

This is called muscle testing, and can be done with just about anything. For example, do you want to know whether a diet soda or a candy bar is good for you? Hold that diet soda or candy bar in your right hand and place it against your heart. Now, extend the left arm and state, "This soda (or candy bar) is good for me." Have your trusted friend try to push down on your arm. See what happens.

Now, back to our "promotion" example. What if, conversely, you thought, "I know that I'm going to get that promotion. I see myself in the new position. I see myself being congratulated by my peers." What

Life is like a mirror and will reflect back to the thinker what he thinks into it.

—Ernest Holmes

chance of getting this promotion do you think you have now? Try the muscle test with this example and see what happens. This may sound a little hokey to you, but I'm here to tell you that it works. Your body doesn't lie. Your body will tell you what strengthens you and what weakens you, and negative thinking weakens you every time.

Are your thoughts and beliefs holding you back, and maybe without you even realizing it?

Do you believe you can have the life of your dreams? Well, remember what Henry Ford said, "If you think you can do a thing or think you can't do a thing, you're right." How do you change your thinking if right this minute you believe that you "can't?" One way to do this is to just do it. I know that sounds way too easy, but you have to decide to believe in yourself. No matter who you are, or where you came from, if you believe you can, you can.

Most multi-millionaires in this country were made after the age of 50. It's never too late to change your thoughts to create what you want out of life. Ray Kroc, the founder of McDonald's, bought his first restaurant at age 57. Whether you start putting the wheels in motion at age 25 or 85, you can still end up living the life of your dreams.

*Life is hard,
and society is hard
and if you don't consciously
prepare yourself each day to
practice wonder and joy, you
get really good at practicing
stress and pain and anger
and anxiety and fear.
Kids laugh 300-400 times a
day. But grown-ups?
Only about 15.*

—Saranne Rothberg,
from *Comedy Cures*

To change your thinking, you must first become conscious of *what* you are thinking. Pay attention to your thoughts. Be the observer. Notice what you are thinking, just notice, without judgment. At first this may seem a little awkward, but try it. When you get up in the morning and are getting prepared for the day, notice what kinds of thoughts you are thinking when you first look in the mirror in the morning. What thoughts are you thinking in the shower? Or on your way to work?

According to Jack Canfield, in his book *The Success Principles*, "Research indicates that the average person—that means you!—talks to himself or herself about 50,000 times a day. Most of that self-talk is about yourself, and according to psychological research, it is 80 percent negative..." Really try to observe your thoughts and do so without judgment. Just observe. Don't be hard on yourself when you realize how many negative thoughts really fly through your head each day. All of us have been there to some degree.

The goal here is to break the cycle. If you look in the mirror every morning and say to yourself, "Oh my, I look awful," you need to catch that and stop it. Put up a note on the mirror that says, "You

The quality of your thoughts determines the quality of your life.

—Rabbi Yehuda Berg

are a beautiful and terrific human being" and read that out loud to yourself every morning instead. Or pick out your best feature and concentrate on that. Put up a note that says, "I have beautiful eyes, or great cheekbones, or a perfect nose, or great hair," or whatever! Break that negative cycle and begin a new, positive one. Start your day in the right direction.

Strengthen yourself and you'll find yourself wanting more and more positive thoughts to move through your head. The reason that this is so powerful is that you attract into your life what you think about. If you keep telling yourself how awful you look in the morning, you start believing it, and who wants to believe he or she looks awful? No matter what we look like in the morning, there is something positive to focus on. We are all divine creatures who are on this planet for a purpose. And every single one of us is beautiful in some way. Focus on the positive.

Try this for a month (some research says it takes at least that long to change a habit). You'll be amazed at how much more beauty you see in the world. When all you focus on, and think about, is the ugly stuff, you see the world through the ugly filter. Try putting the beautiful filter on for a while and see what happens.

It's also important to frame your thinking in an entirely positive manner. For instance, it is far more powerful to be "for peace" than to be "against the war." "The Komen Race For The Cure®" is a far more positive statement than "The Walk Against Breast Cancer." Dr. Wayne W. Dyer, in his book *There's a Spiritual Solution to Every Problem,* quotes Mother Teresa of Calcutta. She was asked during the Vietnam War, "Will you join our march against the war?" She replied, "No I won't, but if you have a march for peace, I'll be there."

You may notice that you think you are thinking positive thoughts, when in fact you are framing them negatively. Notice if this is what you are doing.

Another powerful exercise is to think about a time when you were successful at something. What thoughts were you thinking at the time? Did you know you could not fail? Do you remember thinking, "I can do this" or "I can make this happen" or "If so and so did it, I know I can do it?"

There is also a universal law that says "You attract to yourself what you think about." If you want to lose weight, but all you think about is how fat you are, guess what? You get fatter. If you want to create more abundance in your life, but all you think about is what you don't have, or can't afford, you get more of what you don't have.

I'm not saying it's easy to change your thinking, but when you change your thinking, you will change your life. You have to do the work here. Examine what you are really thinking. Once you begin to shift negative thoughts to positive ones (no matter what your circumstances are right now), the energy shifts and more positive things begin to happen. Lives have been transformed, including mine, when positive thinking won out.

And you do have a choice. Every religious book that I have ever run across states that we were given the gift of free will. Choose to be happy. Choose to create abundance. Choose the life of your dreams. Only you can make it happen!

I'm convinced that our state of well being is really defined by the thoughts that we think. Happy people think mostly happy thoughts. It really is that simple, and for some, that hard. It's hard to think happy thoughts all the time when we've spent our entire lives thinking we weren't pretty enough, or smart enough, or talented enough, or whatever.

So much of what we hear and what we're taught turns out to be false on closer scrutiny. Whether it is expert advice, what you read in the paper, or what your mother told you, if it is important, take the time to figure out for yourself whether it is really true.

—Steven D. Levitt,
co-author of *Freakonomics*

Many of us have lived our lives around false beliefs. Just because someone told you when you were eight years old that you were stupid, or not good at math, or couldn't sing, doesn't make it the truth, even if that person was a parent, or teacher, or other authority figure.

When you hear yourself thinking, "God, I am so stupid," learn to stop yourself in your tracks right now and say, "No, that's not true. I made a mistake. Everyone makes mistakes. I will learn from it and do better next time."

Then, go on with your life.

Many people seem to be masters at beating themselves up. I say STOP DOING THAT! How do you stop these negative thoughts? When you notice that one of these negative thoughts has popped into your head, immediately stop and say, "That's not true. I'm not stupid (or ugly, or fat, or lazy, or...)" and then immediately tell yourself the truth. The real truth.

This even works better if you look into a mirror, look yourself in the eye, and say about 20 times, "I am good enough, I am worthwhile, I am intelligent," or whatever the opposite of the negative thought is.

And saying "I'm not stupid" is not as effective as saying "I am intelligent." A positive statement always carries more power with it.

I could probably write an entire book on how old belief systems affect us, but to sum it up it all boils down to this: Just because someone said it, wrote it, or plastered it on a billboard, doesn't make it so. Challenge your beliefs. Don't buy into old thinking. Tell yourself over and over and over again that God doesn't make mistakes and since He made you, you are not flawed. God didn't create any of us with flaws. We are each perfect, just as we are.

We are no better or worse than anyone else. If people tell us that we are less than perfect, they are operating from an agenda that we really don't want to be any part of. Let them think what they want but don't believe everything they say. Maybe they feel insecure or are trying to manipulate us, or feel threatened by our wanting to succeed. That's their problem. It only becomes our problem when we buy into it. So don't.

Decide today that you are a whole, healthy human being who is just as good as anyone else. Your gifts may be different than others, but you do have gifts. Find them, unwrap them, and share them with others. Know that you are here for a purpose, and whatever that purpose is, it is needed or you wouldn't be here. Then let all the other stuff go. Only give your time and energy to things that make your life better.

If your life becomes better, so will the lives of those around you. You'll be happier, which in turn makes others happier. And think of all the time you will save by no longer playing into those negative beliefs.

Decide today that you deserve to think positive thoughts; that there is a beautiful world around you that is yours to enjoy; that your life can be anything you decide it to be. Choose to be happy.

Yes, that's right, you can choose to be happy. Abraham Lincoln once said, "Most folks are as happy as they make up their minds to be." So decide to be happy. Decide that negative thoughts will no longer cloud your world. Decide on what's important to you and stay focused on that. Decide what your Ideal Life will be and begin living it today.

Don't let the opinions of others get in your way. You know you can do it. Begin to enjoy your gifts and your relationships. Take back your time. Take back your life. Give your energy only to those things that are important to you. By doing these things you'll begin to see that you do have the time and energy to live the life of your dreams.

You'll also begin to use your money only in ways that are supportive of your Ideal Life. You'll

*We change the
world not by what
we say or do, but
as a consequence
of what we
have become.*

—Dr. David Hawkins

be more aware of how you are currently using your money and what changes you can make to begin using it to create and sustain the life of your dreams.

More importantly, as you focus more attention on the things that are truly important in your life, the things that are not important will fade off into the sunset. Through the beautiful colors that the sunset brings to you, you'll be able to begin to realize that it's the stuff that doesn't really matter, that we give so much time and energy to, that gets in the way of us living the life of our dreams.

Give yourself the gift today of looking for the sunset. Let the negative beliefs you have go. Once you've enjoyed the sunset, the next step will be shooting for the stars!

Too many people spend money they haven't earned, to buy things they don't want, to impress people they don't like.

—Will Rogers

CHAPTER 5

Does Your Spending Support Your Ideal Life?

Have you ever joined a weight loss program or know anyone who has? Well, the first thing they ask you to do is an exercise in awareness. They ask you to write down everything you eat in a day. Most overweight people have no idea how much food they are really consuming each day. Many eat for reasons other than nutrition and survival. They eat for comfort, out of boredom, due to stress, when they're sad, when they're happy.

In contrast, most thin people eat when they are hungry, stop when they are full, and aren't attaching emotions to eating, other than pure pleasure and satisfaction, i.e., fulfillment.

Spending has some interesting similarities to eating. Many people spend money for comfort, out of boredom, due to stress, when they're sad, when they're happy. Sound familiar?

Most of us do not spend money only on things that bring real pleasure into our lives and give us a sense of fulfillment. We spend unconsciously just as overeaters often eat unconsciously.

After 25 years of working in the financial planning arena, I can tell you that most of us don't really know where our money is being spent. If I asked you today how much money you spent on food or clothing or entertainment in the last year, would you know? Almost all of us know what we spend on our mortgage or rent payment or car payments. But how much did you spend on birthday or Christmas gifts last year, or things the kids "needed," or soda pop, or car washes, or meals eaten outside the home.

I'm not saying that you shouldn't spend money on these things, but in order to feel fulfilled financially, you must know where your money is going and, more importantly, *why*!

Janet Tyler Johnson

Many of us spend money for purely emotional reasons to try to feel better. Rather than dealing with stress by exercising or meditating, for example, we see that our favorite store has a sale going on and before we know it, we're perusing through the shoe aisle for that fourth pair of black shoes we really "need." Or maybe our girlfriend just dumped us, we have nothing to do on a Friday night, and we think a few new CDs or a set of golf clubs or a new motorcycle might be just what the doctor ordered.

We also live in a society where the divorce rate is sky high. Many children are growing up with parents who no longer live together. Such situations carry with them a great deal of emotion for both parents—anger, sadness, guilt, etc. Even when parents are still happily married and living under the same roof, the same emotions can exist because many couples both work outside the home. We feel guilty that we can't be with our children more or angry that we "have to" work. These emotions are very real and often very strong.

None of us wants to feel bad, so what do we do to soothe our guilt or try to make up for not being there? Well, I know kids who own enough clothes to open their own boutique. Some have every electronic device known to mankind.

Finding Financial Fulfillment

Certainly none of us wants our kids to go without, but let's be honest; how much "stuff" do our kids have out of necessity and how much is out of our own emotional turmoil? And from my experience, kids can read this guilt a mile away. They know just how to play us to get the "stuff" they want. They're intelligent and perceptive. We feel guilty; they think, "the mall."

On a different note, most of us got the message along the way that "he who dies with the most toys wins." I don't know where this thought originated, but the advertisers sure want us to believe it. We think we will feel fulfilled when we finally have the right house, or own the boat, or have a second home, or have the latest, greatest everything (big screen TV, golf clubs, jewelry— pick your thing!). Having beautiful things is great; however, most of us know at some level that all this "stuff" does not buy happiness. Just ask someone who has been diagnosed with a serious illness whether this "stuff" means happiness.

Again, I'm not saying that we shouldn't strive to be as successful as we can and own wonderful things, but if the only reason you want to own the bigger house is that it will be bigger than your neighbor's, or that people will admire you, then guess what? You're setting yourself up for a fall. If you do, on the other hand, want a beautiful home in the mountains because you feel called to live there and believe it will bring a sense of peace to your life, then I say "go for it."

The key is the "*why*." What's important to you, what *you* value.

But maybe it's not the home or the cars that are coming between you and feeling financially fulfilled. Maybe it's the $20 here and $20 there that are being spent unconsciously that, when added up, are preventing you from living the life of your dreams. For example, let's say your dream job requires additional schooling or training and you never seem to have the extra money to pay for this. Do you know why? Is the unconscious or emotional spending depriving you of your Ideal Life?

To really get a handle on where our money goes, we need our own awareness exercise. We need to be totally honest with ourselves and track every penny we spend for at least thirty days to see where our money is going. On the next page is an Annual Cash Flow Worksheet that you can use for manually tracking your money. If you love working on the

Annual Cash Flow Worksheet

	CLIENT	**CO-CLIENT**
Income:		
Salary:	_____	_____
Other Income:	_____	_____
Deductions:		
Taxes	_____	_____
401k Contribution:	_____	_____
Savings:	_____	_____
Other deductions:	_____	_____
Net Income:	_____	_____
Expenses:		
Mortgage/Rent:	_____	_____
Property Taxes:	_____	_____
Property Insurance:	_____	_____
Home Maintenance:	_____	_____
Home Improvements:	_____	_____
Utilities:	_____	_____
Cable & Internet:	_____	_____
Food:	_____	_____
Household Goods:	_____	_____
Clothing:	_____	_____
Child Care:	_____	_____
Health Insurance:	_____	_____
Medical Costs:	_____	_____
Dental Costs:	_____	_____
Life Insurance:	_____	_____
Disability Insurance:	_____	_____
Liability Insurance:	_____	_____
Auto Payments:	_____	_____
Auto Insurance:	_____	_____
Auto Expense:	_____	_____
Auto Maintenance:	_____	_____
Credit Card Payments:	_____	_____
Education:	_____	_____
Other Loan Payments:	_____	_____
Entertainment:	_____	_____
Subscriptions:	_____	_____
Hobbies:	_____	_____
Memberships:	_____	_____
Travel & Vacations:	_____	_____
Holiday Gifts:	_____	_____
Birthday Gifts:	_____	_____
Wedding Gifts:	_____	_____
Charities:	_____	_____
Miscellaneous:	_____	_____
Total Expenses:	_____	_____
Disposable Income:	_____	_____

computer, I would suggest you purchase Quicken® or Microsoft Money®, or check out www.mvelopes.com, an online financial tracking system.

Once you decide on your tracking system, set up all your categories. Use the Annual Cash Flow Worksheet as a guideline, but feel free to add your own categories. I've found that the more detailed you get, the more information you have at your fingertips to create positive changes. For instance, if you know you spend $1,000 per year on lattes at Starbucks, is it worth it to you to keep spending that money? If it is, that's fine, but maybe you'd rather brew your own coffee at a fraction of the cost and spend the difference on something you value higher or perhaps save that money. Or if you knew it was costing you $2,000 per year to buy cigarettes, would that help you to quit smoking?

Again, the categories can get to this level of detail if you wish, but even the broader categories can open your eyes to some spending that you did not even realize you were doing.

Here's something that really works. Once your categories are established, get an envelope that you can carry with you wherever you go, or keep an envelope in the car, one at the office, etc. For 30 days I want you to get a receipt for every penny you spend and put that receipt in your envelope. And I do mean EVERY penny. If you stop at a convenience store to get a newspaper and some bottled water, get a receipt. If you go out on Sunday morning to get a loaf of bread and a gallon of milk, get a receipt.

Then, once a week, take out your receipts and enter your expenditures by the appropriate category into your accounting system.

Do this for thirty days. Then total up your categories and see what you get. Are there any surprises? Is your money going anywhere that you really didn't realize?

Here's a story about a couple I worked with over twenty years ago. They were a young professional couple. He worked in the big city and she worked in the suburbs. They had a beautiful two-year-old daughter, lived in a nice home in the suburbs, and drove nice cars. The couple came to me because both of them were making above-average incomes yet never seemed to have any money at the end of the month. They had a budget and knew they were not living extravagantly, yet they couldn't figure out where all their money was going.

Janet Tyler Johnson

I asked them to start getting receipts for every penny they spent and then writing down each week how much they were spending in each category. At the end of two weeks, the wife called me and said "problem solved." They discovered they were spending an enormous amount of money on take-out food each week.

You may be thinking that two professionals should have been able to figure this out but with two demanding careers, an energetic two-year-old, a home to care for, and all the other details of busy lives, they didn't even think about what they were spending on food. They were picking up dinner every night instead of cooking, which in their minds was justified given their busy existence. But they never added up what it was costing them.

They immediately decided to start grocery shopping more regularly and eat more home-cooked meals. They didn't need to go cold turkey here and never pick up a pizza, but when they saw the impact purchasing take-out food had on their bottom line, they even decided to take their lunches with them to work from time to time.

One of the key points here is that eating take-out every night was not high on their list of important ways to spend their hard-earned dollars. Most of it was unconscious. It was easier. It took less time. But when they measured the cost versus the convenience, it just wasn't worth it to them.

If you'll try the envelope method for thirty days, you may be amazed at where your money is going. But make sure you go into this with the intention of gaining knowledge. This should not start any fights between partners, or cause you to beat up on yourself. Either of those are a huge waste of your time. The tracking exercise is about making things in your life better, not worse. So no judgments here, just the facts. Then, equipped with this new information, you should be able to make better choices on how to handle your money.

Now, after you have entered your thirty-day numbers into your accounting system, use the Annual Cash Flow Analysis sheet to turn these into annual numbers.

This is where you'll see some dramatic things. For example, if you are spending $200 per week on take-out food, that translates into $10,400 per year. That's a big number. If you just cut that number in half by eating home-cooked meals instead of take-out, you would free up $5,200 per year. That pays for a nice vacation, or maybe a nicer car, or could help you start a business, or pay for schooling.

If you decided not to spend that money but chose to save it for retirement, after 20 years that $5,200 per year would turn into $248,151, if you averaged eight percent growth on it per year.

Is there $100 per week you are spending unconsciously? Or even $50? Or $20? Maybe you don't think so. Well, I challenge you, *in fact I dare you*, to take the Thirty-Day Test of keeping every receipt for every penny you spend, and then see where all your money goes. Only through awareness and conscious spending will you find financial fulfillment.

Be in control of your spending; don't let your spending control you!

Finding Financial Fulfillment

The Envelope Story

I have a dear friend whom I have known for over twenty-five years who handles her money better than anyone I have ever encountered. Laura Cardelli has been retired for some time now, but when I met her way back when, she was working for a hospital system. She was a product of the Depression years (barely!), and because of that, she handled money very carefully. She used what is known as the "envelope system."

Do you remember when paychecks were actually cashed every week? Yes, there was a time when people cashed their paycheck, put whatever cash they needed for groceries, gas, food, and spending into their wallets, and only put into their checking accounts amounts to cover major spending like mortgage or car payments. There was a time when many grocery stores and gas stations didn't accept checks. And credit cards didn't become mainstream until the 1970s.

I used to have a Christmas Club account at my bank. In the early 1970s, I would save money out of each paycheck and around mid-November, I would be able to get the cash out of this account to go Christmas shopping. There was no such thing as a debit card, so off I'd parade with about $500 in my purse, ready to tackle the stores. It's scary when you think about it!

When people cashed their checks, they would take their cash home, and those using the envelope system would have a different envelope for each category of spending; i.e., food, clothing, gasoline, utilities, insurance, real estate taxes, vacation, gifts, donations, spending (or allowance). They would take their cash and divide it among these envelopes. This was their way of saying "I'm going to need $50 per week for food" or whatever the category might be. It was more real than just a budget that some of us had on paper. It was a real-life way of handling your money. And if you were good at it, you didn't cheat and start swapping money around. You stayed within your allotted spending.

Laura is a master at this. She has handled her money this way for over fifty years now and is able to stay within her allotted spending amounts. She and her husband have taken some of the most fabulous vacations because they decided at the beginning of the year that a certain amount of their money was going to be put into the vacation envelope. They have lived within their means, and they have lived well. I don't recall a time when Laura ever told me she felt deprived. She knew what was important to her and that was what she spent her money on.

To this day, she allows herself $30 per week for "spending" and often doesn't spend it. She does have an "eating out" envelope, as well as a few other envelopes designated for things she knows she wants to do, like travel and decorating. She's never carried any debt other than a mortgage and car payment because she made this system work.

Today there is a very sophisticated yet simple technology version of the envelope system called Mvelopes. Take a look at www.mvelopes.com for more information.

When your self-worth goes up, your net worth goes up with it.

—Mark Victor Hansen

CHAPTER 6

Creating More Abundance in our Lives

I haven't met anyone yet who doesn't want a life of more abundance. Abundance isn't necessarily just about more money; it can mean being physically healthier, improving your relationships, having more friends, and/or having more fulfillment in your life. Whatever your definition, there are three concepts which have worked in my life that have allowed me to attract more abundance. These are:

Growth   Gratitude   Giving

You must begin to think of yourself as becoming the person you want to be.

—David Viscott, author of
Finding Your Strength in Difficult Times

By *growth*, I mean personal growth. I found in my life that I wasn't able to attract abundance when I wasn't feeling great about myself. I needed to care enough about myself to feel I deserved more abundance in my life.

No matter what your circumstances are right now, take it from me: you deserve all that life has to offer. So what are you waiting for? The Universe is infinitely abundant. It is just waiting for you to manifest your heart's desires.

How do you tap into that infinite abundance and attract it into your life? Everything is made up of energy. Physicists have proven that even the most solid-appearing mass is really made up of tiny particles and sub-particles that are moving constantly. Human beings are made up of energy, and that energy has a vibrational speed that changes depending on a number of variables. One of these variables is what we think. Positive thoughts tend to raise our vibration while negative thoughts tend to slow our vibration.

Attracting more—more health, more wealth, more love, more peace—requires us to raise our vibration. Anything positive that we want to attract to us requires us to be in a more positive state.

We tend to get what we expect.

—Norman Vincent Peale

Conversely, when we are constantly thinking of negative things, we tend to attract more negative things. (Ever have one of those days when everything seems to go wrong?)

Like attracts like. If you really, really want to own a brand-new sports car, you have to create thoughts that make you feel like you already own it. You need to think thoughts like: *"I so love driving this new car. I love the way it handles as I drive around tight curves. I love the way the leather seats feel under my body. I love the red color and all the gold trim on the car."*

You really have to imagine yourself as already owning that car. The energetic vibration of imagining you own the car matches the vibration of actually owning it. The Universe doesn't know the difference between passionately visualizing something and actually experiencing it. We put out the same vibrations whether we are vividly imagining or actually experiencing something. This is why Olympic athletes visualize themselves winning the gold medal, or top professional golfers visualize playing every hole before a tournament begins. To make it happen, they see themselves having already done it. They raise their own vibration to the vibration of achieving the goal.

High achievement always takes place in the framework of high expectation.

—Jack and Garry Kinder

However, most of us spend our time thinking: *"I'll never be able to afford that sports car. Even if I could buy that car, I'd never be able to afford the insurance. What would people say if they saw me driving a car like that? My boss would never give me another raise if I pulled up to work in that car."*

Do you see the difference in the positive and negative thought patterns? Read both again and you can actually feel the difference. One brings you up, the other down.

So, what can we actually do to physically raise our vibration?

Practice meditation. This may take practice but it's worth learning. Meditation has proven itself to reduce stress, improve health, help improve symptoms of depression, and numerous other benefits, including raising our vibration.

Be in nature. Some people really connect with being outdoors. If this resonates with you, visualize having your heart's desires while walking in the woods, or sitting by a lake. Wherever you feel most at peace is a place that helps you raise the speed of your own vibration.

Using affirmations is also a very powerful way to attract things into your life. Affirmations are simply statements that are positive and affirm your intention. To be effective they need to be stated correctly. For example, if my intention is to be prosperous, I don't say, "I WANT to be prosperous." I say "I AM prosperous." I am creating an energy vibration that matches what I am trying to attract. I don't want to WANT. I want to BE, or to HAVE. So, I say out loud, at least 15 times, "I AM prosperous."

If you're feeling a little skeptical, try it, with feeling! I recently took a class on creating more prosperity in my life. For four days in a row, I repeated "I am prosperous" as often as I remembered to say it, 15 times in a row (some say there is magic in the number 15). On the fifth day, I obtained a new client when I wasn't even prospecting for new clients. My phone simply rang with someone asking me if I could work with her. I had raised my vibration by affirming that I already had the conditions that I wanted to attract.

It's actually a little scary to realize how much power you have until you get used to it. And as miraculous as it sounds, once it happens to you a few times, you start to expect it and it begins to feel normal. That's because it is!

I've listened to a vast number of motivational speakers over the years. All of them say that it isn't the smartest, or most privileged, or most educated people who become the most successful. It's those who want it the most. They treat success like it's a given they will achieve it. They don't doubt. They expect nothing less. Failure is not an option. They see themselves being successful. They picture the beautiful home they will be living in, and the great car they'll be driving, and the wonderful relationships they will have. Then they proceed to watch those things appear in their lives.

Ask yourself this: What would you do differently in your life if you knew you could not fail? Put the law of attraction to work in your own life and you can't fail. The Universe wants you to succeed. It's just waiting for you to ask.

If you try these things and have trouble attracting abundance into your life, go back to the chapter on "What Gets In Our Way." There are some suggestions there about things that may be keeping you from attracting more abundance into your life without you even realizing it. Be patient with yourself. Pay attention to not only what you ask for, but how you ask for it (in a totally positive framework). Do you really believe that you will have it, whatever "it" is?

The second thing that has worked for me in attracting abundance is *gratitude*. I express gratitude each and every day for what I already have. There is a universal law that says, "You get what you think about." Therefore, I put my attention on what I have, not what might be lacking. Every night, before I go to sleep, I put my attention on what I am thankful for and list at least five things that I was grateful for that day.

Even when I'm having a really bad day, which we all do from time to time, I can still easily come up with five things I'm grateful for. I just need to look around. I'm grateful for my health, my husband, my step-children, my parents and siblings, my pets, my home, my environment, my optimism, my sense of humor (especially on those bad days), and on and on.

Truly, the only way to get more of anything into your life is to think about it. So I think about my good health, and I get more good health. If I spent my time worrying about getting sick, guess what? I'd get sick. To create more abundance, I think about all the things I have so that I will feel abundant. The more abundant I feel, the more abundance I get.

Again, you're setting up that same "frequency" or vibration to match the vibration of what you are trying to attract.

The third way, and in my experience the most important way, to attract more abundance into your life is by *giving*. Almost every religion around the globe believes in some sort of tithing, giving ten percent of your gross income, on a regular basis, to the people or organizations that spiritually feed your soul, i.e., your church, or an author of an inspirational book, or the National Park Service, etc. There are countless stories in literature and anecdotally on how tithing allowed people to finally attract more abundance into their lives.

I'd like to share a story about something that happened in my own life. About nine years ago I

Giving connects two people, the giver and the receiver, and this connection gives birth to a new sense of belonging.

—Deepak Chopra

Janet Tyler Johnson

decided to sponsor a child from Brazil through the Christian Children's Fund. I saw one of their commercials on TV and thought participating in this program would be a neat thing to do. I signed up to donate $25 per month to this child. Not a lot of money to me, but I found out later that $25 goes pretty far in rural Brazil.

Up until this time, my income had been pretty stable. I was doing OK, but certainly was not earning the salary that I wanted to. Since committing to this one act of generosity, my income has gone up more than I could ever have imagined at that time. I met and married the man of my dreams, I am doing work that I love and feel passionate about, and have never been happier.

Coincidence? I don't think so! Giving sets into motion a number of wonderful things. First of all, you're showing the Universe that you can be trusted with money. Money, in and of itself, is just energy. Energy likes to flow. Giving is how we keep the flow moving in the Universe; we share what we have with others with no expectation of anything in return.

When we start this cycle of giving and receiving, the Universe sees that you are a source of this energy flowing to others and wants you to do more of it, so the more you give, the more you receive, when your giving is from the heart. I have already promised the Universe that ten percent of the proceeds from the sale of this book will be given to the charities of my choice.

I'm going to mention one more thing here to keep with the theme of giving. While giving ten percent of our gross income is an old, spiritual law that leads to abundance in our own lives, giving of yourself is also something that makes this round world we live in a better place for all. I shared the story of how a small sum of money can make a huge difference in the life of a child who lives in a different part of the world, but giving of your time and talents can create miracles.

It's not always easy to measure the impact of what happens when we volunteer our time and share our gifts with others. Small random acts of kindness can have huge effects on people. Just opening a door for an elderly person could prevent them from falling and possibly hurting themselves. Smiling at people, and being thoughtful and considerate, can change another person's attitude (as well as your own).

Have you ever tried walking down a sidewalk, or through a mall, with a smile on your face? People notice, and they smile back. It's amazing.

While manifesting physical items of abundance into our lives is wonderful, so is attracting feelings of joy and love. You have to make the first move. Whether you are trying to attract more money into your life, or more peace, or more joy, or better health, it starts with you. First you give, then you receive. It doesn't work any other way. If you want more, you need to give more. If you want your child to be happier, show your child how happy you are with her. If you want your husband to be more loving, be more loving to your husband.

Yes, it takes a little thought and effort on your part to make the first move, but if your taking action comes back to you tenfold (or as some say a hundredfold), what are you waiting for?

Imagine the world we would be living in if we each gave first, then waited to receive. There is no limited amount of abundance in the Universe that we need to compete for so feel free to give. You'll be amazed at the result.

Abundance is available to you whenever you decide you want it. Give to others, be grateful for the abundance you already have, be specific in asking for what you want, intend to receive it, and then enjoy. You deserve it!

Finding Financial Fulfillment

The Leukemia Walk

I'd like to share a story with you about the power of giving of yourself, not because I want to get any credit here, but because a wonderful group of people I am proud to know took an idea, ran with it, and created a miracle. This story depicts the amazing things that can happen when people give from the heart.

In 1996, a co-worker of mine, Karla Nodorft Heller, sent out an email where we worked asking for donations for a walk to raise money for leukemia research. I lost a sister, as did she, to this disease, so obviously her email sparked my attention. She told me that she and her family were headed to the Mall of America in Minneapolis where the fundraiser was to take place. I asked her why they were going all the way to Minneapolis to do this (we lived in the Madison, Wisconsin area, which was a five-hour drive from Minneapolis). She told me that Madison did not have any activities aimed at raising money to find a cure for leukemia.

My first thought was that we should do something about this. I went back to my office and called the local chapter of the Leukemia & Lymphoma Society and was told that they did hold a walk in Milwaukee once a year, and there were some other types of events held in the state, but nothing in Madison.

Karla and I decided to meet with the chapter representative and see if there was something we could do in the Madison area to help raise money. After meeting with this gentleman, we decided that a walk would be something we could do. It wasn't competitive, so operationally it would be easier to organize than a race. We also decided that New Glarus, Wisconsin would be our venue. We felt by holding the walk in Madison it might get lost among all of the other events that take place in a larger city.

One of the miracles of this story is that New Glarus is a wonderful town known as "Little Switzerland." It was founded by Swiss immigrants in 1845 and currently has a population of around 2100. Karla and I initially met with the Chamber of Commerce to ascertain if a walk was something the village would get behind. We knew we would need the cooperation of the people of the town to make this work. Well, lo and behold, not only did we get their support, but two individuals immediately offered to help us organize the walk. We then talked with the town officials as we knew we would need police and fire department support. We needed permission to get our route marked off and closed to transportation during the walk so no one would be injured. I've never seen anything like it, but this quaint little town totally embraced our idea.

Karla's parents immediately volunteered to work with us and opened their home to us for some of our initial meetings. We formed a committee, and the rest, as they say, is history. We will be celebrating our tenth year in 2006, and have raised over $500,000 to help fund research and patient aid.

The National Leukemia and Lymphoma Society was so impressed with what we did our first couple of years that they decided to make our walk the model for the entire nation. Two hundred and seventy-five walks just like the one in New Glarus are now held every year around the country and over $29 million was raised in 2005.

Again, I can't take any credit for this other than having had an idea and acting on it. It's the committee members, the local businesses, and the people of the town itself who have made this event such a success. We were given free advertising by the local newspaper, one of the local radio stations broadcasts every year, and local celebrities now attend to help us get even more exposure around the state.

When you have a passion to help others, miracles occur. I'm sure many people feel that a lot of blood, sweat, and tears went into making the New Glarus Light the Night Leukemia Walk successful, but compared to a lot of other things I've been involved with over the years, the walk seemed to kind of fall into place. The right people appeared to get the work done, get the sponsors, and get support from local businesses to make it happen. I personally never talked with anyone who said "no" when asked if he or she could help. It truly has been amazing.

I can't begin to tell you how much abundance came into my life after giving of myself with this event. My husband came into my life, bringing with him my three precious step-children, we began building the house of our dreams, and I'm now living in this house doing work I love and feeling very fulfilled. It's no coincidence that the first caused the second.

The story of this event shows you that if you have an idea for helping others, share that idea with someone else and see what happens. And always keep in mind that if your heart is in the right place, and you put the interests of others first, you truly can accomplish extraordinary things. I will always be grateful to the many people who acted on our original idea and laid the groundwork to make the Light the Night Walk for Leukemia & Lymphoma a national success! You know who you are and it never would have happened without you!!!

The thief to be most wary of is the one who steals your time.

—Anonymous

CHAPTER 7

Finding More Time to do the Things that Fulfill Us

We've all read the books and attended the seminars on "life balance." If your life is anything like mine was a while back, though, it's hard to fathom how you're ever going to get enough TIME to create any balance. Between long work hours, a commute, kids, cleaning, shopping, etc. etc., who has time for balance? And the deeper you're buried in the demands of life, the more impossible it seems to be able to dig your way out.

My solution was to make a big change. I quit my corporate job and started my own business. Before I did that, however, I did a lot of planning. I had 24 years of experience in the financial services industry before I decided to make this change.

One of the issues that caused me to make this change was that I wanted my life back. I did a lot of soul searching. I completed many a mind map on my values and what I wanted my Ideal Life to look like. The beauty of mind maps is that you can always do a new one as you begin to grow and your outlook begins to change. And for several years (and I did work on these issues for several years), I tweaked my maps, created new ones, and I still think my Ideal Life is a work in progress.

After all, isn't that the definition of life to begin with? I can't imagine getting to a place and saying, "Well, this is it. I'm THERE!" What, nothing to look forward to? No new adventures in store for me? I'm done? This is as good as it gets? I don't think so.

Taking small steps, which I did over a period of years, led up to this "big change," which in reality was just the last of many, many small steps. Quitting a high-paying job may look like a big step to others, but to me it was just the culmination of a lot of planning, both financial planning and life planning.

Janet Tyler Johnson

I turned fifty years of age about two weeks before I turned in my resignation at my corporate job. Reaching that magical age seemed to give me a new lease on life. I don't know exactly why, but I felt that being fifty gave me permission to do a lot of things that I wouldn't previously have done. I was excited about entering a new decade in my life with new things on the horizon and wanted a new professional start to go with it. I had this book in me for several years but didn't have the time or energy to sit down and write it. I decided I needed to take back my life, do the things I loved and ONLY the things I loved, and create a life filled with fulfillment.

It took me about three months to de-stress enough to begin to realize that all of the hobbies and fun stuff that I used to have in my life had gotten pushed to the back burner. It was really no one's fault but my own. When I commit to something, I give it about 200 percent. While working at my prior job, my life was consumed by my work. I problem-solved on the way to the office in the morning. I worked at home in the evenings and on the weekends. I followed a great recipe for "life unbalance," and when things got so bad that I feared it was going to affect my health, I said "enough is enough." Life is just too short to spend your time living someone else's agenda. I needed my own agenda. So, I created a home and work environment that could support the life I want to live and it's working out better than I ever could have imagined.

I tell you all of this because maybe you see yourself in my story. I was tired. I was slightly depressed although I didn't really realize it. I was surviving, but certainly not living, and definitely not living up to my full potential to use the gifts that God gave me. So where did I start?

First, I took a weekend when I knew I would have some time to myself and got out my pencil and paper. It was a beautiful summer day. There is nothing I like better on a day like that than to sit in my chaise lounge on my beautiful deck and soak up some rays. I relaxed for a while, meditated and then began to get creative. I created a mind map called "My Ideal Life." I thought of all of the areas of life: work, play, health, spirituality, relationships, and giving back, in each area played around for a while with what would be "my ideal" in each of those areas.

Without a doubt, my biggest challenge was my lack of TIME to be able to do all of the things I wanted to do. My job was taking up way more time in my life than I wanted. I began immediately to mentally scale back on some of the hours I dedicated to work, i.e., less work on the weekends, etc., but that wasn't getting it done. So, I did what I always do: I went to the bookstore.

Getting Things Done

I came across some of the best material I have ever found on getting my life back in control: David Allen's *Getting Things Done*. It is not a time management book. It is a "getting your life back under control" book. I can't in these brief pages do justice to Mr. Allen; there's just too much great stuff. But I will give you a few ideas that may immediately help you feel like you're getting a little more control back in your life.

I'm sure you've heard the statement that sometimes the simplest of ideas carry the most power. Well, this did it for me. Mr. Allen recommended that you find a small shirt pocket or purse-sized pad of paper and carry it with you at all times. I found a terrific miniature composition notebook that works just fine at an office supply store. You can invest a little money and get a great tiny leather notepad cover that comes with a notepad and pen at www.levenger.com.

Finding Financial Fulfillment

So, you might ask, what is so great about carrying this notepad around with you? Well, it's about finding a way to clear out all the things in your head that you try to remember each and every day. "Don't forget to pick up a gallon of milk on your way home." "Suzy's soccer game is on Thursday night at 5 p.m." "I really need to find a new pair of shoes to go with that new suit I bought." "I have to remember to call the Smiths about setting up an appointment with them." "I have to get in touch with that vendor to make sure we'll have what we need for that big presentation we're doing." "Don't forget to call the dentist." Etc., etc., etc. Every single day, our brains are just cluttered with things that we need to remember to do.

And where are you physically located when all of a sudden you remember, "Oh gosh, I have to pick up milk on the way home"? Usually you're sitting at your desk; you're not at the grocery store. When things to do pop into your head, you need to remember, WRITE THEM DOWN IN YOUR NOTEBOOK! Get them out of your head. (David Allen's book explains all the procedures you can follow on how to best handle all of these notes to yourself about things you don't want to forget.)

Using my little notebook has been a great way for me to stay focused on the things that need to be done right now, while knowing that I won't forget about the things that need to be done later. If, in the middle of the afternoon, I think about needing to pick up milk on the way home, I pull out my little notebook, start a grocery list, and then immediately go back to what I was doing.

Then, as soon as I hit the grocery store, I pull out my notebook. If, when in Aisle 3, into my head pops a thought about remembering to call a client to set up a meeting to touch base, I pull out my little notebook, make myself a note, and continue my shopping. I can concentrate on the task at hand, knowing that when I get back to my desk, I will pull out my notebook and jot a reminder on my calendar to call the client I thought about in Aisle 3.

Nothing gets lost and my concentration level goes way up. I'm no longer cluttering my memory with things to try to remember; I'm focusing on the thing that needs my attention at the present moment.

Having a notebook, and using it, might sound like such a small thing to you but believe me, the amount of energy using this simple tool frees up is amazing. We spend an inordinate amount of time each and every day just trying to keep track of all kinds of stuff in our heads. That translates into having a lot less time to go do something fun, or having the space in our brain to create something really great at work, or just being able to really pay attention to what our second grader is trying to tell us about her day at school.

An important key here is that you need to make sure this notebook is small enough to carry with you no matter where you are, i.e., working out or going to an elegant, black-tie affair. You might just get a great idea in the middle of the dance floor.

While doing research for this book, I read that a great idea stays with us for, at most, about forty seconds. If that is indeed true, you'd better hightail it off the dance floor for a second, make a note, and then get back to socializing. Perhaps this sounds a little crazy, but believe me, once you get in the habit, it really works. I never have to worry about forgetting things anymore; my little notebook travels everywhere I do.

Janet Tyler Johnson

Cleaning Up Your Personal Environment

Now that you've cleaned out the clutter in your head, it may be time to clean out the clutter on your desk, in your home, in your garage and basement, and anywhere else you tend to accumulate things.

Be honest, how do you feel when you've thoroughly cleaned out a closet? Don't you feel like some great weight has been lifted off of your shoulders? How about when you finally decide to clean off your desk? Don't you feel less distracted and more able to concentrate on one task at a time?

Again, David Allen in *Getting Things Done* has some wonderful tips on how to keep your desk clean and tidy and produce more work than you ever thought imaginable, with less stress to boot! Better yet, some of his principles can be applied to every aspect of your life.

Does your car look like a family of twelve has been living in it? If you have a long commute or travel a lot in the car for business, or you're the mom or dad in the neighborhood who always seems to be giving someone else's kids a ride home from soccer practice, your car may be a disaster zone. Perhaps you've never thought of this before, but surrounding yourself with clutter really zaps your energy. If you don't believe it, try it for yourself. Completely clean out your car and see if you don't feel better driving it than you did surrounded by things that don't belong there.

The same goes for every room in your house. Even if your home is immaculate, having too much stuff tends to gunk up the works. I enjoy cooking more when my counter tops are clean and clear. I feel better in the morning when I step into a clean bathroom, with a clear vanity and everything in its place. When my bedside table begins to get overrun with books to read, bottles of hand lotion, and any other number of things, I feel boxed in. And every time I look at that bedside table, I get distracted with the thoughts of how I really should clean it off and get some of that stuff put away.

I have lived in homes that are bigger than what I need, that felt open and airy. I've also lived in tiny apartments where I had a hard time fitting in everything I owned. Can you figure out which place felt better to live in? In which environment do you think I could be more creative? And which place was easier to clean and maintain?

Clutter gets in our way—physically, emotionally, energetically, spiritually. You might think that having a lot of stuff around you feels cozy and comforting, but there is a fine line between cozy and feeling confined, even trapped. We all love to be surrounded by things that have meaning for us and that bring us joy. But when you can't find a place to put down a magazine because the coffee table is overflowing, or you're afraid to open the closet door for fear of what may fall on your head, it's time to get rid of the clutter.

Creating for yourself a wonderful environment, both at home and at work, can also save you tons of time. When you have a pile of papers on your desk just begging to be filed, isn't is more time consuming to have to go through that pile to find something you need rather than opening up a desk drawer, going to the file, and putting your fingers on it in a matter of seconds? Or what about in your garage? You need a hammer. It's not where it should be. Your garage looks like it had been hit by a tornado. How long does it take to find the hammer?

Do you see the point here? Being neat and organized is a huge time-saver. It may take a little work in the beginning to get everything "in its place," but once you have, and keep it there, life from then on gets easier. There is no bigger waste of time then needing something, having to go look for it, and an hour later finding it, or having to run out for a replacement. If it was where it should be in the first place, there's another hour back in your life to do something a lot more fulfilling than scouring your home, office, car, or whatever, for the missing item.

If your entire environment needs an overhaul, go gently and slowly. Start with a drawer, or your desk, or your kitchen. One thing at a time. Get creative about your organization. Think about how things could best be set up to serve you. Or, if you're really not good at this at all, think about hiring a professional organizer. They exist, and they specialize at systems and designs to help you create efficiency in your life.

Make it a ritual that each month you'll spend half of a day reorganizing some part of your environment. You'll really be amazed at how little time it takes to get yourself organized. And once you get organized, you'll be motivated to keep it that way. Going back to the old, cluttered way of life will just not feel good to you at all.

If you have a hard time getting started, think of it this way. There are a lot of people out there who are a lot less fortunate than you and who could really use an old pair of winter gloves, or a shirt that no longer fits you, or dishes you never use. Make it a part of your ritual to intentionally see how much stuff you can come up with to give to others. Also, the value of the items you donate to a charity may be deductible on your tax return. So, it's a win, win, win situation. The person in need receives a gift, you give yourself the gift of more time and energy, and possibly the gift of less taxes to pay at tax time.

Maybe one of the most beneficial reasons to get rid of clutter is, by doing so, you create space for new, better things to come into your life. When your clothes closet, for example, is filled to the brim with old clothes you no longer wear, there is no space for new, better clothing. And looking at the old clothing, day after day, actually drains energy from you. Decide today to get rid of the old and make space for the new. You'll feel so much more energized, satisfied, and fulfilled!

Learn To Say "No"

OK. We've now beaten the clutter thing to death. What other things can we do to help us gain more time in our lives? Many people feel totally stressed simply because they have too much on their plate. Too many obligations. Too many commitments. Maybe it's time to make a list of things that you currently are involved in, i.e., business-related activities, church activities, school activities, etc., and see if it isn't time to pare things down a little.

We all love to feel needed, and it's sometimes very difficult to say "no" to a worthy cause, but believe me, you won't be doing anyone any good if you are stretching yourself too thin. If there is a cause you feel passionate about, or a group that you feel drawn to, that's great. But don't you want to be in good enough shape to be able to give the things and people and activities your all?

Sometimes, when we are overcommitted, we try to offer our time and energy, yet never quite feel like we are doing a good job at anything. One important thing to remember is that you only have so much energy. And the amount of energy you have may not be the same as someone else's. You really need to gauge for yourself what is a healthy amount of time to devote to any specific thing or things.

Taking on too much is really a recipe for disaster and sometimes even for illness. When your energy gets too depleted, your body will tell you when you've been running on empty for too long, and if you don't do something about it, it will.

So how do you keep from getting overburdened? You start by being totally honest with yourself and deciding how many commitments you can take on. If you are raising small children, you may not have the time or the energy to take on many, or any, other commitments.

If your job is demanding, you work long hours, and you have little or no time for your family, taking on a volunteer project may be out of the question, unless you are willing to cut back at work a little or involve your family in your volunteering.

Many of us just aren't good at saying "no." But you need to get better at this. You need to be able to set some boundaries for yourself. Know what your limits are.

If you want to live the life of your dreams, you can't be running around like a crazy person giving all of your time and energy to things that carry little or no meaning for you. You really need to get in touch with what is important to you and then begin to adjust your time accordingly.

For instance, if you've been a member of the church board for the last five years and you feel like you've given it all you can give, maybe it's time to step back and let others have the opportunity to give.

Most likely they will bring some fresh ideas to the table and have the energy and enthusiasm that you had back in the beginning. However, if you feel you are still making a difference, and being part of the board is meaningful for you, then by all means stay.

Maybe there's something else you're involved in that just doesn't have the pizzazz that it used to for you. You'll know what to give up and what to take on, as long as you are being honest with yourself about your own motivation.

I belonged to a professional board for several years where one member was bound and determined to stay forever. It was apparent to the rest of us that she did not want to relinquish her power (which really was her "perceived" power, as none of us really had any power just because we were board members).

It took several of us to approach her to discuss what a wonderful thing it was that she had given so many years to this board. We told her we appreciated all her hard work, but raised the idea that, by her staying on the board, she was preventing someone else from enjoying the same experience. She finally agreed to go and we tried to make it as positive as possible.

Janet Tyler Johnson

All of us have to remember that in situations like this it is easy for our egos to get in the way. We feel important and necessary to the group. Yet, in reality, maybe we are in the way of someone else coming in to the group who can offer more energy, time, and passion for something that has gotten somewhat stale for us.

Do some soul searching when it comes to your own list of activities and have the courage to step aside if your passion and energy have waned. Your leaving can become a great gift to the group if you're no longer able to give all you once did. So, maybe the gift to yourself is to say "no" sometimes to allow you to really give your all to the things you say yes to, and not spread yourself too thin.

The whole notion of saying "no" is about self-care. Many of us do not do a good job of taking care of ourselves. We're too busy trying to take care of everyone else in our lives. Self-care should be at the top of our list, not the bottom. It's similar to saving money. If you don't pay yourself first out of every paycheck, but wait until the end of the month to pay yourself, you often don't have anything left at that point. You need to care enough about yourself to ensure you are meeting your savings goals, and to take care of you.

If you've ever flown in an airplane, the flight attendant always announces that in the case of an emergency in which the oxygen mask drops down in front of you, first put on your own oxygen mask, then take care of your children or others around you. Self-care needs to be given that same priority. If you don't make it a priority to eat right, exercise, and pamper yourself from time to time, it won't happen.

For you to have the energy you need to create and sustain the life of your dreams, and take care of your loved ones, you need to take care of yourself. You can't get so busy doing stuff that doesn't matter that you don't have time for the things that do. You will give yourself the gift of more time if you take care of yourself, stay organized, and focus only on the things that matter to you. Let everything else go.

People often ask me how to "let everything else go." My answer is to do so politely and with great compassion, but just do it. Stop worrying about things that you have no control over. Stop getting anxious about things that will probably never happen. Keep your thoughts positive and productive and focused on the things that are important to you.

Some people need a little practice at this, but others just say, "That's it. I'm not giving that situation one more ounce of my precious energy. I'm just not going there any more!"

Time is something we never get back. Do whatever you can to be positive, manage your time, eliminate the things that deplete your energy, and increase the things that give you energy and feed your spirit. Keep your thoughts on your Ideal Life. You'll not only improve your life, but you'll improve the lives of those around you.

Hope for the best, prepare for the worst.

—Anonymous

CHAPTER 8

Building a Solid Financial Foundation

I would be remiss in my role as a Certified Financial Planner® professional if I didn't have some discussion on the basic financial components that comprise a solid foundation upon which to build financial security.

Why is it so important to have a solid financial foundation in place? And how does this relate to living your Ideal Life? Maybe the following story can answer those questions for you.

Finding Financial Fulfillment

Several years ago, a woman called to set up an appointment to see me. Her daughter, whom I'll call Sally, just lost her husband and needed some financial advice. We scheduled a time to meet the following day.

Sally was a 40-year-old mother of three who had been married for eighteen years. Her husband had died unexpectedly at the age of 42. Sally hadn't worked outside the home in fifteen years and had not handled any of their financial affairs. She needed some help in sorting out her husband's retirement accounts, and wanted to know what to do with the life insurance proceeds she had received.

Her husband had been earning about $100,000 per year. The life insurance proceeds were $200,000. His retirement plan contained about $60,000. (Although he earned a nice income, he had been in sales and had changed jobs quite often, which was why he had a relatively small retirement plan given the number of years he had been working.)

It was obvious to me that Sally was very distressed. She and her husband had a lifestyle like many Americans; big home, big mortgage, nice automobiles, went on nice vacations, and only one income. When her husband died, the income ended. In her eyes, not only had she lost her best friend, her whole world had just fallen apart. Intuitively she knew that there wasn't enough money to support her and her children in their current lifestyle for very long, and in just two years her oldest child would be heading off to college.

Sally did not want to go back to work. She hadn't worked in fifteen years. She loved caring for her home and her children and really viewed that as her calling. She said she had very few marketable skills, and she felt she was needed at home as she still had a child in elementary school and two in high school. Sally also wanted to continue to live in the house they were in as she felt that her children needed the stability.

From a financial planning standpoint, her situation was dire. Her house, with the big mortgage, made up a huge part of her monthly expenses. Downsizing to cut her costs made sense from a financial planning perspective but she did not want to do that. She also didn't want to work outside the home. We met several times to discuss these issues and it was very apparent that she was emotionally in worse shape each time we met.

After a few meetings, I gently suggested that she see a therapist for some grief counseling. She could not make any decisions and yet something needed to change. She either needed to cut expenses or increase her income; otherwise she'd be out of money in two to three years.

This story illustrates what can happen when people don't want to deal with building a solid financial foundation. Sally's husband, given their circumstances with him as the sole breadwinner, should have had more like $1.5 million in life insurance rather than the $200,000 he had. Sally then could have invested the $1.5 million, which at a six percent return per year, would have provided her with $90,000 per year in income. Because this planning had not been done, Sally was not only left with inadequate insurance proceeds, but she was forced to make some big financial decisions at a time when she was emotionally distraught.

I usually advise people, after the death of a loved one, not to make any major decisions for at least a year, but in her case we didn't have that kind of time. She needed to do something now.

While the building blocks of a sound financial plan may, at times, seem unpleasant to talk about or deal with, ensuring that your financial foundation is solid is one of the best gifts you can ever give your heirs. The last thing you want your loved ones to have to do is make tough financial decisions at a time when they are emotionally in one of the worst times in their lives.

On a lighter note, I once worked with a young married couple just starting their lives together. We were discussing how much life insurance each of them needed. We talked about what they would do if one of them died, i.e., would they stay in their home, or downsize to a condo, for example. I wanted to know what they expected their future expenses would be so we could provide them that lifestyle if one of them died.

After much discussion, the wife finally turned to me and said, "Janet, just make sure that if he dies first, I have enough money coming in to grieve in the Bahamas."

She was kidding about the Bahamas, but was very clear that she didn't want to be left in a situation like Sally's, and neither did he if she died first.

The following is a list of the building blocks needed for a solid financial foundation. The list is not meant to be all inclusive; each individual should seek professional advice to ensure that his or her personal financial foundation doesn't have any holes in it. However, the following items apply to most people. Included is a short definition of each component, and, if warranted, some brief recommendations.

At the end of this chapter, I've also included a checklist so that you can check off each item as you complete it.

1. **Last Will and Testament**:
   Everyone needs a will. A will is an instrument that declares how you direct your assets to be distributed at your death. Even if you have established trusts (see "trusts" below), you most likely still need a will. State laws vary so you should consult an attorney to get a will prepared and to make sure it conforms with the laws applicable in your state. By the way, if you don't have your own will prepared, the state you are living in has one for you. Unfortunately, you may not like how THEY decide your estate should be divided.

2. **Trusts**:
   There are two basic kinds of trusts: *Revocable Trusts*, where you can change the provisions of the trust prior to your death, and *Irrevocable Trusts,* in which the provisions cannot be changed. These can be valuable instruments to

help reduce estate taxes, control how distributions are made, or provide income to dependant or special needs children, among other things. Again, an attorney who specializes in estate planning should be consulted as to whether these make sense for your particular situation.

3. **Pre-Nuptial Agreement**:
"Pre-nups" are not just for the rich and famous. They're also not merely for "divorce planning." A pre-nup is very useful in second (or third) marriages where you want to establish what assets were yours prior to the marriage. This can ensure that your heirs will receive your assets upon your death and prevent everything you have from going to a second spouse upon your death, and ultimately their children, leaving your own children out in the cold.

In this society where people are living longer, it is getting more common that people in their 60s and 70s are marrying for a second or third time. I've seen ugly and expensive court battles over estates simply because no planning prior to the marriage was done. If you want your children or grandchildren to get your collection of art, or Grandma's diamond ring, make sure you have a pre-nup in place showing that these assets were yours prior to the marriage, and whom, upon your death you wish to receive them.

4. **Health Care Power of Attorney**:
   This is a directive where you indicate how you would like to be administered to should you become unable to make medical decisions for yourself, such as whether or not to insert a feeding tube, or be put on a respirator. It also includes whom you appoint to make medical decisions for you. It's important that you name someone you know will carry out your wishes despite what they may want to do. We've all heard of cases where people's lives are basically in the hands of the courts, sometimes for years, because no such written directive was in place. Most hospitals now carry the blank forms, or you can get them from your physician or local and state agencies.

4. **Financial Power of Attorney**:
   This directive appoints someone to handle your financial affairs should you become incapacitated. Again, this is an important document. Mortgage payments, car payments, and other bills still need to be paid should you end up in the hospital or an assisted living center in a condition where you are unable to write a check or make a financial decision for yourself.

   Most of us who are married have joint checking accounts where either spouse can sign a check, but in some households, each person may also have a personal checking account in which the other spouse does not have signing privileges. What if that money is needed? And what if you are single? Who can get at your money if you're unable to?

But beware, once you have appointed someone, through this document, to be able to handle your financial affairs, they can legally sign for you at any time and have access to your money. A Power of Attorney is a very powerful document. Be very careful to whom you give this power.

5. **Disability Insurance**:
Most people today are not adequately covered if a disability occurs that prevents them from earning income. And if they do have some type of disability coverage, it usually doesn't totally replace the amount of money they were earning.

How long can you go without income? Or with only part of your income?

It can be extremely difficult to get disability payments from Social Security. I once worked with a woman whose husband began losing his eyesight. He lost his job due to this and did not have disability insurance through work. He was down to about twenty percent of his vision, unable to drive or do much of anything for that matter, when she applied for disability through Social Security. They denied him.

The fact that he still had twenty percent of his vision disqualified him from receiving any payments; he wasn't "totally" disabled by their definition at the time. He eventually did qualify as his vision further deteriorated but the payments he received did not equal the amount of income he had been earning. She was forced to get a second job just to try to keep a roof over their heads and food on the table.

6. **Life Insurance**:
In my opinion, in today's economy, life insurance is needed for only two reasons: 1) to replace income in the case of a premature death when assets have not yet been accumulated to support a family or a business partner, and 2) in estate planning situations where life insurance is used to offset estate taxes. That's it!

Life insurance used to be sold, and sometimes still is, as a great way to "save money." It used to be popular to use a life insurance policy to save money for retirement, college funding, etc. And in many cases, when you could earn twelve percent tax-deferred on the savings component of the policy, it might have made sense for some people (especially those who had only small amounts of money to save).

There weren't many places you could get that kind of growth on $25 per month. But that was 20+ years ago and times have changed. Interest rates have dropped, and in those old policies, you aren't earning twelve percent any more. Of course, times may change again. Due to our current low interest rate environment, insurance companies are designing new products. Some of these may end up being fabulous, many may not.

My career began in the insurance industry, although I haven't sold a policy in over ten years. As a financial planner, I see abuses every day of what was intended to be a great solution for people who hadn't yet built up enough assets to be self-sustaining. Many people have been taken advantage of over and over again and some are actually insurance poor. (They are paying way too much in premium dollars for what they are getting as a benefit.)

I can't stress enough how important it is to have someone independent that you can trust review your policies and see if any changes are warranted. You might find yourself saving a bundle just by getting a good, qualified second opinion! (Seek out a Certified Financial Planner® professional who acknowledges to you in writing that he or she acts as a *fiduciary*. A fiduciary is legally bound to put your interests before his or her own. This is a good start to finding someone you can trust to work with.)

7. **Auto Insurance**:
   Most states require auto insurance if you own a car, or at least liability insurance in case you are at fault in an accident. If you haven't had your policy checked for a few years, it might be worth sitting down with your agent and making sure the coverage you have is adequate.

8. **Homeowners Insurance**:
   There are a couple of things with homeowners insurance that are very important to have on your policy. One is replacement coverage. Make sure you will receive benefits for what it would cost to replace your home AND the contents of your home. Another area to look at is whether you have valuables such as jewelry, silver, artwork, furs, collectibles, etc. covered under a separate rider. Most homeowners policies limit the amount of coverage to fairly small amounts for items such as these. And you may receive a discount if you install a fireproof safe in which to keep jewelry and collectibles.

9. **Liability Insurance**:
   People are suing for more and more these days and many people carry relatively small amounts of liability coverage. The cost for liability coverage is very low compared to how much you could lose if you were sued and found at fault. While most auto and homeowners policies include liability coverage, often the amounts are not adequate to cover your entire net worth. Additional liability insurance can be purchased through an umbrella policy, at very reasonable cost, that will cover you in addition to any liability coverage you have on your other policies.

10. **Long-Term Care**:
Most people today are familiar with this relatively new form of insurance. Long Term Care can cover nursing home, assisted living, and home health care expenses. This insurance varies greatly between carriers for cost and benefits. It's something that should be thoroughly investigated before purchase. Also, the financial strength of the carrier needs to be looked at closely.

Healthcare costs are escalating at an alarming rate and claims being paid from these types of policies are still relatively recent. There isn't a lot of data as to how much the claims on these types of policies will affect insurance companies in the future.

As with any type of insurance policy, the financial stability of the insurance company is extremely important to evaluate. Again, working with an independent financial planner can be an advantage in evaluating these types of coverage rather than just working with one agent from one company. Shop around. Look at coverage available through associations like AARP or professional associations you may belong to. Also, group policies are beginning to be offered by employers, all of which help in keeping the cost to the consumer down.

11. **Business Insurance**:
    If you own your own business, there are many additional types of insurance that you may need. Meeting with an agent who specializes in these types of coverage is important. Also, if you run a business from your home, you need to make sure you have adequate coverage. For example, if you have an office in your home, and you have a fire or flood and lose everything, your business assets will probably not be covered under your homeowners policy.

    It's important to find out how your insurance company handles such types of claims. Don't assume you will be covered just because your office is in your home, or even on the same property as your home. You may not be.

12. **Emergency Fund:**
    The old rule of thumb was to have at least three to six months of income sitting in a safe, liquid investment where it was readily available if you had an emergency, i.e., lost your job, had a leak in the roof, etc.

    I don't always agree that you should keep that much money just sitting around earning little or nothing. However, I say that assuming you have all of your insurance needs covered (house, car, life, disability). And you still need this money liquid. But, after almost 25 years in the financial services industry, I have seen very few people who have actually ever had to use this money in an emergency.

The "cost" of having half a year's salary earning next to nothing for twenty years is extremely high. An alternative is to have most of this money properly diversified and invested in liquid investments (like mutual funds, index funds, or exchange traded funds) where you still have the ability to earn something if you don't ever need the money, yet have it available if you do.

Now, if you follow my suggestion, you must also realize that there is some risk attached to this strategy. You may need the money when the stock market is down and you would be taking a loss on your investments if you need to sell them to get the cash. However, in my way of thinking, if you truly need the money for an emergency, then it is an emergency.

Keep in mind that this is just a suggestion. If it makes you feel better to have this amount of money in the mattress, buried in the backyard, or in money market funds, that's up to you. Just keep in mind that it could easily cost you $100,000 or more over twenty or thirty years if that emergency never happens.

13. **Safe Deposit Box or Fireproof Safe**:
It's important to have a safe place to keep important papers such as a list of policy numbers and the company names for all of your insurance policies. Don't keep the actual policies in the safe deposit box. In the event of your death, your heirs may not have access to it, which could delay payments being made to your family. Paper policies can

always be replaced, but you do need to keep a list of policy numbers safe.

You may also want to keep safe certain items of jewelry that could not be replaced (Grandma's engagement ring that she gave you), stock certificates, birth certificates, passports, deeds to property, titles to cars, and other things of that nature. You can keep a copy of your will in your safe deposit box or safe, however, your executor should have a copy as well as your attorney. This way, if no one other than you has access to the safe deposit box or safe, your will can still be probated without any delay.

14. **CD, Mini-Drive Storage, or Online Safe Deposit Box**:
In addition to or in lieu of a safe deposit box (and this won't work for Grandma's engagement ring), you can scan all your important documents into your computer and then keep a copy of them on a CD or portable disk drive. You can store the CD in your safe deposit box. There are now portable disk drives that go on a key chain.

I like the portable disk drives better than a CD for backup storage because you can take them with you wherever you go. They are about the size of an old fashioned pack of gum.

There are also services out there now that keep copies of these documents for you in an "online vault or lockbox." While these may sound like scary options, if something happens to your computer or if you are traveling out of the country and lose your passport, for example, having a backup copy of your birth certificate, social security card, and other such identifying documents, either on a portable drive or in an online vault, can save you a lot of hassle!

15. **Backup System for your Computer**:
More and more of us are keeping important documents, family photos, contact information, our calendar, and our financial information on our computer. Think for a minute what would happen if your hard drive crashed and you lost all of this vital information.

Here is a relatively new solution that saves me a lot of time as it backs up on the fly. It's a personal backup server and is available at a very reasonable cost. Unlike backing up to CDs or tapes, this system backups your data constantly. That means you are never exposed to times when your data isn't backed up.

I bought one for my business computer and found that the same company offers very affordable backup servers for personal computers. Check out www.mirra.com. (You can do a Google search to see if there are other companies that offer the same type of product.) The Mirra server I bought was very easy to install and use. It backs up what I'm doing in real time; no need to do a special backup procedure at night or some other scheduled time.

If you've ever been through a hard drive crash, you know the horror of losing things, and maybe not even remembering everything that's on your hard drive. I had it happen once and hope never to go through it again. Again, a little "insurance" offering some peace of mind.

16. **Online or Manual System for Tracking Cash Flow**:
    I devote a whole chapter to this so I won't go into too many details, but I can't say strongly enough: you will never feel financially fulfilled if you don't know where your money is going and why. Awareness is everything. Your spending decisions must be conscious. If you truly are using money to support your life, you won't use it for purposes that are in conflict with your values, i.e., spending out of boredom, or reducing stress, or getting a "high." You will use your money to enhance and improve your life, and to create the most amazing life possible.

17. **Record of all Policy Numbers, Passwords, etc.**:
    I already mentioned that you could keep a list of insurance policy numbers in your safe deposit box or in a fireproof safe in your home. An alternative is a software program called *Passwords Plus*. Very inexpensively, this program stores all your passwords for websites, email accounts, online financial accounts, etc., as well as insurance policy numbers, bank account numbers, credit card

numbers, frequent flyer miles, etc. It's an amazing, easy-to-use program that keeps all this data in a password-protected file. (You'd better not lose THIS password, but it's the only password you need to remember!)

There are probably numerous programs like *Password Plus* out there, but this is one I stumbled across and decided to purchase. The advantage I've found is that I have a copy of this program on my PC, as well as a copy on my PDA. Now, no matter where I am, I have all the data I want at my fingertips.

Do you ever need your spouse's social security number when opening a new bank account, or applying for a loan, or whatever? Well, I don't know about you, but I don't remember all these numbers, nor do I want to clutter up my memory trying to. You do have to be careful that you don't give access to this program to anyone you don't want having it. Your "whole life" could be in here if you get detailed enough. But, no more sticky notes, no more cheat sheets, now you have everything in an organized fashion, in one place. It's amazing how much memory you can free up in your own brain by knowing this information is safe and at your fingertips, freeing up those brain cells for other creative endeavors. Try it, you'll like it!

18. **Statement of Final Wishes or Directives for Family to Follow**:
    We discussed earlier the importance of having a will. However, often the will is not read until after the funeral or memorial service is over, so this may not be the best place to list any final directives. A separate statement can be used to list any final wishes or instructions that you would like carried out. It is not a legally-binding document but rather a final message to those you leave behind.

    For example, let's say that at some point you decided that you wish to be cremated rather than buried. Or that you want some particular piece of music played at your memorial service. Maybe you have a certain cemetery picked out as your final resting place. Or maybe you want to leave letters to your spouse and children telling them how much you love them and how much they have meant to you. It's important that we tell someone, or maybe several someones, that in the event of our death, we have sealed envelopes containing our final wishes and where we've left them for safekeeping. Personally, while no one ever wants to think about dying, many of us just don't express to our loved ones often enough how much they mean to us. If you're in a family where things like that just aren't said much, write your feelings down. Imagine what a wonderful legacy you are leaving to people you care about.

Those are some of the financial basics that can help you build a solid foundation for creating the life of your dreams. It may look like a lot, but if you tackle a little at a time, it won't take long to really get your financial house in order.

If this seems like an overwhelming task, or something you really don't want to take the time to do, then hire a Certified Financial Planner® professional and he or she will do a lot of this work for you. It would also be worth it to have a financial plan prepared. I have never run across anyone who built a house without first having a plan drawn up (they call them blueprints ☺). Think of a financial plan as the blueprint to your life.

Once you make sure your money and values are aligned, you're off to a great start to begin living an incredibly fulfilling life.

Never put off till tomorrow what you can do today.

—Lord Chesterfield

the Center for Fulfillment and Prosperity

JATAJ

Financial Basics Checklist

- ☐ Will
- ☐ Trusts (if needed)
- ☐ Pre-nuptial agreement (if needed)
- ☐ Health Care Power of Attorney
- ☐ Financial Power of Attorney
- ☐ Disability Insurance
- ☐ Life Insurance
- ☐ Auto Insurance
- ☐ Homeowners Insurance (including replacement of dwelling and contents)
- ☐ Liability Insurance
- ☐ Long Term Care
- ☐ Business Insurance (if a business owner)
- ☐ Emergency Fund
- ☐ Safe Deposit Box or Fireproof Safe
- ☐ Online or Manual Tracking System for Cash Flow
- ☐ Backup system for computer documents, family photos on computer, etc.
- ☐ Record of all important policy numbers, passwords, etc.
- ☐ Statement of final wishes or directives for family to follow

www.jataj.com
©2006 JATAJ. All rights reserved.

*Knowledge itself
is power.*

—Francis Bacon

CHAPTER 9

Understanding Investing Fundamentals

There is a tremendous amount of information available today on how to manage your investments. I've worked in several areas of the financial services industry in my career and would like to acquaint you with some general truths. I'd also like to disclose that I have in the past, and still at present, manage assets for a fee for clients. Let me say from the beginning here that there is no one "best" way to manage your assets. There are several "best" ways. I know that adds to the confusion for you, but you are a unique individual with unique goals and dreams.

Finding Financial Fulfillment

The amount of risk you are willing to take, the amount of money you are saving, and your long-term objectives all play into the equation. I strongly urge you to work with a financial advisor, preferably a Certified Financial Planner® professional who has been trained to look at your entire financial picture, not just your investments.

To really evaluate how your investments are doing, you have to look at what your investments earn after all costs and fees of investing are deducted, and after taxes. It's not what you earn that is important, it's what you keep. So, with that in mind, let me share some ideas with you that might serve as guidelines, not only when choosing someone to work with, but also as to what methodology may best serve your needs.

The "big picture" way of looking at investments is that you can invest in stocks, bonds, and cash. There are all kinds of investment choices today, i.e. mutual funds, managed accounts, exchange traded funds, hedge funds, investment trusts, government securities, CDs., etc., but most are still made up of stocks, bonds, and cash, or some combination of those.

There are also more complicated investments that include futures, options, derivatives, etc. I'm not going to get into a detailed discussion of all of these instruments. You can go to the internet today or to any bookstore or library and find out all kinds of information on various investments and how they work. I'd rather discuss some fundamentals that may help make things easier for you to discern how your money should be invested to be in alignment with your values and financial fulfillment goals.

Fundamental #1:
Be Clear About Your Investment Goals

You must know what you are trying to accomplish with your money before you set out to invest it at all. For instance, is the money for your retirement? Or to help get your kids through college? Or to fund a career change for yourself? What is the goal? What time frame are you looking at?

If you're investing money in the stock market to try to make a killing in the next two years so you can quit your job and start a business, you are taking a very big risk. The stock market is not, in my opinion, for gamblers or short-term investors.

Remember the term "day-trader?" Day-traders were individuals who traded stocks day in and day out, in and out of the market, trying to make a few dollars here and a few dollars there, in the hopes of making a lot of dollars over a very short period of time. I know of individuals who quit their jobs, took their 401(k) money, and sat at home in front of the computer buying and selling stocks all day long, each and every day.

The vast majority of them are back in the work force, basically starting over after having lost everything. Some are even trying to get out of a huge pile of debt because they not only lost money in the markets, but they lost money they borrowed to trade in the stock markets. Sounds scary, but it was more common than you think during the "tech bubble" days.

This is not to say that you, as an individual, cannot on your own make money in the stock market. It's how you go about it that counts. Know what your goals are, what your time horizon is, and how much risk you're willing to take before you even begin investing your money.

Janet Tyler Johnson

Fundamental #2:
Diversify, Diversify, Diversify

Diversification is key. Have you ever heard the expression "don't put all your eggs in one basket?" Betting everything you have on one stock, or even a few stocks, can be very risky. Owning just small company stocks, or stocks of only US companies, or just large company domestic stocks can also be a risk.

The secret to diversifying your investments is to slice up the investment world just like you would slice up a pie, with each piece of pie representing something different. For example, one piece could be international stocks, one piece could be domestic (US) small company stocks, and don't forget mid size and large size US stocks, real estate, commodities, corporate bonds, government bonds, or municipal bonds (if you are in a high-income tax bracket), and cash-type investments such as CDs or money market funds.

Your investment allocation is very important. According to all the experts, how you allocate your investments (how much is in stocks, how much is in bonds, and how much is in cash) accounts for the vast majority of your overall investment return every year. Therefore, it is very important that you work with someone who can help you allocate your investments across these multiple asset classes, keeping in mind the amount of risk you are willing to take, your overall time frame, and the goal you are trying to achieve.

As you can see, there are a lot of things to think about when it comes to investing your money, which leads us to another topic that I think is paramount for you to consider.

Fundamental #3:
Rebalance Your Portfolio

Another critical component to your overall investment success is rebalancing your allocations in your portfolio. By this I mean that if, when working with your financial planner, you agreed that your allocation should be 65% stocks, 30% bonds and 5% cash, and a year later, through market movement, your portfolio contains 75% stocks, 20% bonds and 5% cash, then you own more stocks than your original allocation called for and are taking on more risk than you agreed you would be comfortable with.

Conversely, if a year after that your portfolio has 55% stocks, 40% bonds and 5% cash, you are now invested more conservatively than you may need to be to meet your investment goals.

The markets move all the time, sometimes moving up or down quickly in very short periods of time. It is important that you keep your portfolio invested to your original allocation in order to increase your probability of investment success.

How often should a portfolio be rebalanced? There is no hard and fast rule on this topic, but from all the studies I've read over the years (and the academics look at this question in depth), I recommend to clients that we rebalance any asset class in the portfolio, i.e., international, small company, large company, real estate, bonds, etc., that is more than 25% above or below its target.

For example, using the scenario of the international stock allocation, if you owned 20% international stocks in your portfolio, when that allocation reached either 15% on the downside or 25% on the upside, it would be time to rebalance.

Setting up a parameter like this also helps take the emotion out of investing. We, as human beings, have a hard time letting go of our winners. It's easy to get greedy, or just hopeful that we'll make even more money than we have. It's also hard to purchase something when it's losing value.

But remember, the one simple truth about making money in the stock market is to buy low and sell high. Since our human nature makes this difficult, setting a parameter of a 25% change in your allocation makes rebalancing easier to do.

Fundamental #4:
Know What It's Costing You To Invest

How much is it costing you to invest your money? There is no free lunch out there, even though sometimes it appears that there is. Every type of investment has some form of cost attached to it. When you purchase a stock, you are charged a commission. When you purchase a bond, the broker buys the bond at one price, marks that price up, and then sells to you at the higher price (sort of like buying at wholesale and selling at retail price).

All mutual funds, index funds, and exchange traded funds have charges called "expense ratios." In addition, when buying exchange traded funds you also pay a commission. Some mutual funds carry sales charges in addition to their expense ratios. Investment advisors and investment managers charge fees to manage your portfolios for you.

To make things even more complicated, there is no one best way of investing for everyone. Stocks may be the appropriate choice for some investors, while index funds may make more sense for others.

Regardless of which type of investment is best for you, in my opinion, it is critical that you KNOW what your investments are costing you. I've seen investment portfolios where the cost of investing is in the 3% per year range. Well, if you can reduce the cost by even one percent each year, you could be saving yourself hundreds of thousands of real investment dollars over a long period of time.

Let me give you an example of how costs impact your investment success. If you are 25 years old today and are saving $2,000 per year in your 401(k) plan, you continue to do this until you are 65 years old, and you average 9% growth on your money over that time period, a 1% "cost" (9% versus 10% that you could have earned during those 40 years) amounts to $224,164! You would have accumulated $932,453 at 10% per year, and $708,289 at 9% per year. That's almost 25% less money for you to use during retirement with just a 1% difference in growth over the entire forty years. So, if you think a little thing like a 1% difference in cost doesn't matter, you might want to think again.

Whoever you are working with to handle your investments should be able to tell you exactly how much it is costing you to invest. If they won't disclose this information to you, you may be better served by someone else. Reducing the costs of investing can mean far more money in your pocket, and that's what counts!

Fundamental #5:
Don't Forget Taxes

I always tell clients, it's not what you earn on your money that's important, it's what you keep. We've already discussed costs and how they can erode your returns. Well, taxes can also have a large impact on your overall investment success. The money you pay in taxes on your investment earnings is money you will never get back.

In an investment vehicle like a 401(k) or an IRA, your taxes are deferred (delayed) until you actually begin taking distributions. Then, 100% of what you take out is taxable just as if it was income. In taxable accounts where you save after-tax dollars, every year you are taxed on any profits that you have had to report. For example, if you sell a mutual fund that had a gain in it (a profit), the gain is taxed in the year of the sale. You may be eligible for capital gains treatment where the amount of tax you pay is lower than your ordinary income rate, but it's still tax that has to be paid.

A good investment advisor or financial planner will do everything he can to offset taxes for you each and every year. Of course, you can never totally eliminate taxes, and reducing taxes should not be your number one priority if it means you would have to change your asset allocation to either take on more risk or reduce the amount of growth your portfolio is likely to achieve. But taxes are important.

If you do have to sell something that has had a gain that would be taxable, often times you can sell something else in your portfolio that has had a loss to offset that gain.

Of course, it is critical that you work with your tax advisor when trying to do this. I mention tax reduction as being important as I have seen many, many brokers and advisors over the years completely ignore the tax ramifications of making changes to a client's portfolio. Again, it's not what you earn that is important, it's what you keep. And, you should always look at returns after all fees and taxes have been deducted. That tells you how your money is really growing.

Being diligent in this area can potentially mean thousands and thousands more dollars in your pocket. Make sure your investment advisor effectively tax manages your money.

In summary, having clearly defined goals, properly diversifying and allocating your money, rebalancing periodically, reducing your costs, and managing your taxes are important components of achieving financial success. If this all seems a little overwhelming, go to the Financial Planning Association's (FPA) website, www.fpanet.org, to find a Certified Financial Planner® professional in your area. The FPA is the professional association for the financial planning community and their website, www.fpanet.org contains a variety of free resources from brochures on "How to Pick a Planner" to free online advice from a CFP® professional.

When choosing a planner to work with, interview at least three planners, if possible. It's important that you find someone with whom you feel comfortable, who wants to understand your values, and help you align your investment strategy with the things you value the most. If you do, you'll have a valuable ally in your quest for financial fulfillment.

There are only two lasting bequests we can give our children... one is roots, the other wings.

—Stephen Covey

CHAPTER 10

Teaching Our Children about Financial Fulfillment

We all want our children to have the best lives imaginable. So, how do we teach our children about money, what money represents, and how they should handle money in their lives? Obviously the best gift we can give them is to SHOW them how to handle money. If we set the right example, they will learn valuable lessons. We all know that children model us. They look at what we do, not necessarily what we say.

So what behaviors around money are you teaching your children?

Ask yourself this question: What is my first memory of money? Ponder that question for a while. What was the first experience you can remember where something about money impacted you? Were you a small child? An adolescent? A teenager with your first job? If you can come up with an honest answer to that question about your first memory of money, most of you will see a pattern as to how you handle money today. Was your first memory one of abundance? Scarcity? Being swindled? Not being able to afford something? Getting paid money for something you didn't want to do, i.e., clean your room, finish your Brussels sprouts, taking out the garbage?

How did your parents handle money? Does the behavior you saw in them affect how you handle money today? Most of us have very vivid memories of how our parents handled money. If you're a Baby Boomer, money may not have been discussed in your household. And having no communication around money in itself can affect how you act around money today.

A friend and colleague of mine, Carol Nowka, told me a wonderful story of her first memory of money. She grew up in a farm community. The local fair was a big deal to kids in the area when she was growing up. She was a very little girl at the time and had saved her allowance for months so when the fair was in town, she could enjoy herself at the arcade. She vividly remembers walking the entire game area twice to make sure she picked a game she could play. She spotted a swimming pool that was filled with toy ducks. The sign said if she picked a duck she would win a prize. Above the pool hung beautiful dolls. Well, she picked her duck, handed it to the man working the booth, and he handed her a small jumping bean. She asked what it was and he said it was her prize. She pointed up to the dolls and he said no, the bean was her prize.

Well, needless to say, she was very upset. Here was a small child who did what she thought she needed to do to win a a doll and now she felt totally betrayed. Carol told me that to this day she doesn't trust salesmen. She always thinks they're out to take advantage of her. She realized that the perceived facts are not always as they seem, and incomplete information can be one's downfall. On the positive side, however, her arcade experience taught her that there is "no such thing as a free lunch."

Finding Financial Fulfillment

Isn't it amazing that all of those "lessons" came from that one experience, and that over five decades later, she is still affected by an event that happened around money? Did you realize that experiences like Carol's around money can hold so much power for so long? They can operate very subconsciously so that you don't really see what is motivating you to act in a certain way.

If you're willing to spend a little time thinking about how you handle money, and what in your past might be related to such attitudes and behaviors, perhaps you'll realize that you've been operating from a place that isn't really coming from your true self.

Your behavior could be based on a reaction to something that you saw growing up or something that happened to you. Maybe one of your parents was a big spender and couldn't support himself in retirement because he never saved a dime. As a result, you are a penny pincher. Or, the opposite may have happened. Maybe one of your parents would never spend money on anything and you felt deprived, so now you are trying to make up for it by buying anything you want, whenever you want.

I encourage you to explore your past experiences with money and see if anything from "way back

Janet Tyler Johnson

when" has any bearing on how you handle money now.

With all that said, what are your children learning from you and how you handle money? Is money something you don't talk about at home? Are you subtly letting your children know that you think people who have great wealth came by it dishonestly? Are you showing your children that giving to those less fortunate than you are is important? Are you even aware of the messages you are giving them around money?

As I said earlier, actions speak louder than words. If you are killing yourself working 80 to 100 hours per week just so you can give your kids a beautiful house to live in, and fancy cars to ride in, and the greatest, latest gadgets, I can tell you that those very kids have come to me and asked me to teach them how to manage their money.

They don't want to raise their kids the way they were raised. They want to earn a good living, save for the future, but also be able to spend time with their kids. They remember that what they wanted most from their mom and dad was TIME with them. They didn't want the stuff. Yes, they thought the big house was nice, but it didn't replace having Mom and Dad around, and they don't want to duplicate their parents' behavior.

I once did a workshop after which two women in their mid-twenties came up to me and begged me to teach them how to handle their finances so they didn't get into such a trap when they had kids. They wanted balance in their lives and they wanted to give their kids a great environment to grow up in, but not at the expense of never seeing their kids.

So these two young, single women wanted to start saving now to make sure they had what they needed later on. And they wanted options. They didn't want to get trapped in a job they hated just to make enough money to support their lifestyle. I could see from the desperation on their faces that the messages they had received when they were growing up caused them to want to act in an entirely different way than their parents had. I give them a lot of credit for wanting to explore these things at such an early age.

I don't write about all of this to create any guilt for you. Maya Angelou said "We make decisions on what we know, and when we know more, we make better decisions." Well, for you the game has just changed, because now you know more.

Janet Tyler Johnson

If you have children, it might be time for you to sit down with your kids and undo some of those messages you gave them without knowing any better. Now that you do know better, you have the power to improve things no matter how old your children are. Also, keep in mind that you really don't have as much power over your children as you think you do. They still are their own little persons who also make decisions based on a whole variety of things.

If your children are grown, keep in mind that maybe somewhere in their past one of their teachers, or a neighbor, had a huge impact on how they handle money today. Or, maybe it was the guy at the fair who caused them to act the way they do around money.

So what do you do to help your children get good money messages? And when do you start? For older children, check out www.moneyinstructor.com. There is an abundance of information there on everything from how to write a check to economic theory.

For younger children, I'd recommend Money Savvy Generation at www.moneysavvygeneration.com. Money Savvy Generation was founded by Susan Beacham in 1998. Today, she and her husband operate this business together. Their mission is to help children visually learn how to handle their own

Finding Financial Fulfillment

money. They have created a piggy bank and a cow bank made of a see-through material and divided into four separate compartments: Save, Spend, Donate, and Invest. Each foot has a cap on it that can be unscrewed to get the money out. The banks are terrific.

I started putting my loose change in my bank and I can't tell you what an impact it had just approaching the piggy bank and having to decide into which compartment my 83 cents was going to go. Or should I divide it? I had to make a decision then and there. And because the words Save, Spend, Donate, and Invest stare you in the face, you are forced to think about what would be the best thing to do. It doesn't let you just save money without thinking about its function.

As a child, I can remember having a piggy bank and it was all about spending. I was saving long enough to buy something in the future that I couldn't afford now. Well, the Money Savvy Generation bank gets you thinking differently. It doesn't let you forget that donating and investing, for example, are also part of the picture. It's not just all about spending.

My first 83 cents went into the "donate" compartment, simply because I decided then and there that it was money I didn't need. It had just been lying around in a desk drawer. So why not give it to someone who needed it more than I did? Boy, it felt so good to do that. I had set the intention that I'm going to help someone else.

The moral of this story is that the Money Savvy Generation bank is designed to help kids handle their money in better ways and should probably be sitting on all of our desks or dressers or nightstands. We all have ways in which we can handle our own money better. We need to be aware and conscious of our decisions, and because we now know more, we make better decisions.

Just imagine how this could work in your own life. Could you go to bed at night knowing that the only compartment in the bank that had any money in it was the "spend" compartment? And those other three compartments were empty and staring you in the face? So much for denial. Sometimes it is the simplest of things that are the most powerful.

Order one of these today and try it for yourself. You'll truly be amazed.

The best thing you can do to help your children feel more fulfilled around money is to SHOW them how well you handle your own money. Show them that you are not wasteful. Show them that you only truly buy what you need, not just what you want at the moment. We live in a society of such immediate gratification that I know this is difficult, but IT IS DOABLE!

Talk with your kids about who they would like to donate money to. Maybe a charity that's important to you isn't important to them. Kids tend to want to help other kids. Suggest sponsoring a child in another country and have your children donate part of the money from their allowance, or birthday money, or whatever. Have them draw pictures for this child, or write letters to him or her. I do this and both my step-daughters and the sponsored child are enriched!

Or maybe your kids are animal lovers and you can have them collect aluminum or other recyclables to cash in and donate the proceeds to the local Humane Society.

There are thousands of good causes out there. Make giving a priority and give you and your child the gift of helping others. It will help build your child's self-esteem, bring your family closer, and may make a huge difference in the life of someone far less fortunate than you are.

Don't just take my word for it. Try it!

Financial fulfillment comes from a sense of knowing that your money and your values are in tandem. You feel full, not empty or like something is missing in your life. You know that the money you earn, save, invest, and donate is supporting the things you value. Help your children learn this feeling early in life. It may be one of the most important gifts you ever give them.

*If one advances
confidently in the
direction of his dreams,
and endeavors to
live the life which he
has imagined,
he will meet with a
success unexpected in
common hours.*

—Henry David Thoreau

CHAPTER 11

Summing It All Up!

We've come to the end of this journey. By now you should have lots of ideas about feeling more in control of your financial situation. You know how to build a firm foundation and you know where your money is going. You have even begun to match your money with your Ideal Life. You are using money as a tool to enhance your life and bring you more meaning and fulfillment. You're investing in a way that cuts costs and taxes, which means more money in your pocket.

You've developed a very clear picture of what your Ideal Life looks like. You know where you are headed and have begun to take steps to manifest that

Ideal Life into reality.

You also are attracting more abundance into your life. Wonderful things, even mystical, magical things, are happening in your life. You're feeling more positive and energized because you are using your energy only in the ways that support your Ideal Life. You've learned to control your time better, which leads to having more energy. You've helped your children begin to understand that meaning, not money, is everything. They are watching you bring more meaning into your life and notice that you are happier, calmer, and more at peace than you've ever been.

If some or all of the above is not happening yet for you, then I suggest you reread parts or all of this book again and continue doing the exercises. Our journey together has included learning new skills, and new skills are not mastered overnight. They must be practiced over and over again to become second nature to us.

As you begin to master these new skills, they get easier to perform. Keeping yourself organized, for example, is not something that you do once and you're done. It's an ongoing process. And it's easy to slip back into the old way of doing things. That's

OK. If that happens, go easy on yourself. Remember that it took years and years to perfect the old way of doing things; it may take a while to be consistent in your new way of operating.

Life is a journey. Success is a journey. Happiness is a journey. The skills it takes to create fulfillment are worth pursuing. Take it from one who's been on both sides of this fence: fulfillment is MUCH better!

Money in and of itself is neither good nor bad. Having money can be great. Using money to enhance your life, the lives of those you love, and the lives of people you may not even know, is a wonderful thing. Everyone I know has some type of issue around money. Money is something that touches us at very deep levels. It brings out our fears, reminds us of old wounds, and sometimes lets the worst in us emerge.

How you view money in your life is really up to you. How you use money can make all the difference in your life. Using it to alleviate boredom, or reduce stress, or just trying to feel better usually leads to an empty life and an empty bank account. However, using money to create something positive and life enhancing and giving money to help enhance other people's lives can be magical.

Remember that money is really just a thing. By

itself, it holds no power. We give it power. And you have the choice to be frivolous with it or to be a great steward. Be conscious about your money. Use your money with great intention. The Universe really does want you to live a fabulously abundant life. Show the Universe that you can handle it. And when the magic starts pouring in, enjoy every minute of it!

Thank you for spending some of your precious time with me on this journey. I hope you got as much or more from reading this as I did from writing it. My hope is that each and every one of you apply these skills to your own life. Nothing happens in this world without action. So get moving! The sooner you start, the sooner you'll get there. And this side of the fence is truly a beautiful and wondrous place to live. You really shouldn't miss another minute of it!